LEARNING THE
HARD WAY

Learning the Hard Way:

The Leadership Experiences of Lieutenant Agar Adamson during the South African War, 1899-1902

Craig Leslie Mantle

CANADIAN DEFENCE ACADEMY PRESS

Copyright © 2007 Her Majesty the Queen, as represented by the Minister of National Defence.

Canadian Defence Academy Press
PO Box 17000 Stn Forces
Kingston, Ontario K7K 7B4

Produced for the Canadian Defence Academy Press
by 17 Wing Winnipeg Publishing Office.
WPO30247

Library and Archives Canada Cataloguing in Publication

Mantle, Craig Leslie, 1977-
Learning the hard way : the leadership experiences of Lieutenant Agar Adamson during the South African War, 1899-1902 / Craig Leslie Mantle.

Includes bibliographical references and index.
Issued by: Canadian Defence Academy.
ISBN 978-0-662-45312-3 (bound).--ISBN 978-0-662-45313-0 (pbk.)
Cat. no.: D2-191/1-2007E (bound)
Cat. no.: D2-191/2-2007E (pbk.)

1. Adamson, Agar, b. 1865. 2. Canada--Armed Forces—Officers--Biography. . South African War, 1899-1902--Biography. 4. South African War, 1899-1902--Participation, Canadian. 5. Command of troops. I. Canadian Defence Academy II. Title.

FC553.S6M36 2007   968.04'8092   C2007-980068-8

Printed in Canada.
1 3 5 7 9 10 8 6 4 2

Acknowledgements

Although the cover of this short book reflects a single author only, I would very much like to thank a number of fine colleagues and excellent historians who freely offered their time and expert counsel. Colonel, Dr. Bernd Horn, the Director of the Canadian Forces Leadership Institute, provided the encouragement to take this project to its fullest fruition. I am truly thankful for the opportunities that he has afforded and to him my most sincere appreciation must be given. I should also like to thank Major, Dr. Doug Delaney and Major John Grodzinski, both of the History Department at the Royal Military College of Canada, for their useful suggestions on earlier iterations. The same must also be said of Professor Carman Miller of McGill University. Their collective efforts helped to improve the pages that follow and my only remaining hope is that some day I will be able to return the favour in kind. Mr. Martin Hubley of the University of Ottawa, whilst in England over the summer of 2006, sacrificed his personal time to search files of interest at *The National Archives of the United Kingdom*, in Kew, Surrey. Although his researches are not reflected in the endnotes to this volume – despite his best efforts, nothing that could be used was found – I am indeed grateful for his effort and willingness to assist.

I feel fortunate in having been able to bring the mapmaking skills of Mr. William Constable to bear on this volume. His manipulation of my less-than artistic sketches – nothing more than a series of pencil lines on hotel stationery – into professional maps is truly appreciated. My thanks are also extended to Corporal Lee Ramsden of the Lord Strathcona's Horse (Royal Canadians) and to Lynn Bullock of the Princess Patricia's Canadian Light Infantry for providing some of the photographs that lend support to the text. The staff at the *Library and Archives Canada* in Ottawa and the *Glenbow Museum* in Calgary aided immensely in granting access to both textual records and period photographs. Warrant Officer Marc Bourque of the Canadian Defence Academy, as always, answered what must have seemed to him like a flood of technological questions, all of which he answered capably and without complaint. My sincere appreciation must also be given to the staff of the 17 Wing Publishing Office, especially Captain Phil Dawes, Evelyn Falk and Adrienne Popke.

A much-condensed and less-advanced version of this volume was earlier presented at the 17th Military History Colloquium in London at the University of Western Ontario in May 2006. I wish to thank the many conference participants who offered their opinions on the presented work, both during the question period and later in informal conversation.

And as always, I must thank my wife Angela, for without her varied help, this book would not have been possible.

Table of Contents

List of Maps ii

Foreword iii

Preface v

Introduction 1

Learning the Hard Way 11

Map and Image Credits 99

Select Bibliography 101

Glossary 103

Index 105

Author's Biography 111

List of Maps

MAP 1: South Africa, 1899-1902. .31

MAP 2: The Battle of Wolve Spruit, 5 July 1900.
Sketch 1: The Approaching Battle. 38
Sketch 2: Splitting the Force. 39
Sketch 3: The Strathconas Prepare. 40
Sketch 4: The Strathconas Advance. 41
Sketch 5: Concluding Movements. 42

MAP 3: Movements of Strathcona's Horse, mid-1900. 56

Foreword

I consider myself honoured in having been approached to write the Foreword to *Learning the Hard Way: The Leadership Experiences of Lieutenant Agar Adamson during the South African War, 1899-1902*. I commend this brief and interesting volume to all of Canada's soldiers, sailors and air personnel, in addition to those in the general public who are simply interested in military leadership and military history.

This book serves two distinct, yet important, purposes. First, it speaks to the leadership of Agar Adamson during his formative years as an untested lieutenant. This thorough review, in which both his abilities and shortcomings are discussed, highlights certain timeless lessons that remain relevant even today. Adamson's experiences in South Africa – his fears, his desire to succeed and his determination to "press-on" in the face of adversity – are not all that different from our own and we would do well to observe how he interacted with his soldiers during periods of crisis *and* calm. Although he may have demonstrated particular weaknesses at times, such as being too hasty in battle and remaining somewhat distant and aloof from his brother officers, he has important lessons to teach that will make better leaders of us all.

Second, *Learning the Hard Way* is a milestone publication for it represents a significant contribution to the literature on the South African War, especially from the Canadian perspective. Rarely have the experiences and capabilities of a junior officer received so much attention as they do here. Studies such as this provide a glimpse into the nature of leadership at some of the lower levels of command during a particular place and time.

In many respects, this study presents a minor commentary on the military culture of late-nineteenth and early-twentieth century Canada.

I am confident that everyone who reads *Learning the Hard Way* will uncover something of value. For some, this volume will further their understanding, and thus their appreciation, of our military past. For members of the profession of arms, the following pages will offer varied insight into leadership and human behaviour that may assist in their development as leaders as they progress through their professional military careers. Regardless, I commend this book to all and sincerely hope that it is enjoyed.

Sydney Valpy Radley-Walters
Brigadier-General (ret'd)
C.M.M., D.S.O., M.C., C.D.

Preface

Despite the constant and at times extreme changes that our world is experiencing today, one can take some comfort in the fact that certain things, thankfully, remain immutable. While the nature of operations that Canadian personnel have been called upon to perform has changed drastically from the end of the Cold War to the present, some of the basic tenets of leadership have not. Any examination of leadership in past conflicts, be they modern or ancient, is bound to uncover distinct similarities to our own day.

I therefore recommend this short volume to those who are charged with the responsibility of leading Canada's men and women into danger, whatever it is and wherever it lies. Although *Learning the Hard Way: The Leadership Experiences of Lieutenant Agar Adamson during the South African War, 1899-1902* is about one officer in one conflict, his successes and failures stand as invaluable teaching tools for individuals at any rank level in any of the three environments of today's Canadian Forces. The means to maintain morale, motivate subordinates, ensure disciplinary standards and reward exemplary performance deserve our constant attention regardless of where we are in our professional military careers. Hopefully all who read the pages of this book will come away with something to think about, to act on or merely to discuss with others. This book does not have all the answers to every challenge, but it is an additional resource that I trust you will enjoy and find useful.

And finally, I commend this volume to all who are interested in Canada's military past and in leadership in general. Investigating those personalities who have so far escaped the collective efforts of historians truly provides further insight into the conflicts that ultimately shaped the nation. All in all, *Learning the Hard Way* offers a valuable analysis of one such individual who, after all was said and done, influenced the course of history in his own distinct and particular way.

Colonel, Dr. Bernd Horn
Director
Canadian Forces Leadership Institute

1: Agar Adamson as a young sportsman in Ottawa, *circa* 1885 (back row right).

2: Agar dressed as Napoleon Bonaparte for a costumed ball in Toronto, 1898.

3: Donald Smith, Lord Strathcona and Mount Royal, the regiment's benefactor and Adamson's obliging patron.

4: Lieutenant-Colonel Sam Steele, Commanding Officer, Strathcona's Horse. Agar thought very little of the man.

5: Troopers of Strathcona's Horse making their way to South Africa. Some of these men would eventually serve under Adamson.

6: Rifle practice aboard ship. Such training while en route to the seat of war was beneficial for learning the rudiments of soldiering, but little could here be learned about fighting on horseback amongst rolling hills.

7: The officers of Strathcona's Horse. Adamson would make their acquaintance after arriving in South Africa and would ultimately label them a "very mixed lot."

8: Strathcona's Horse encamped at Cape Town.

9: Sergeant Arthur Herbert Lindsay Richardson with his Victoria Cross.

10: On active service.

11: The outside of a hospital. While Boer bullet and shell took their toll, disease was a much greater threat.

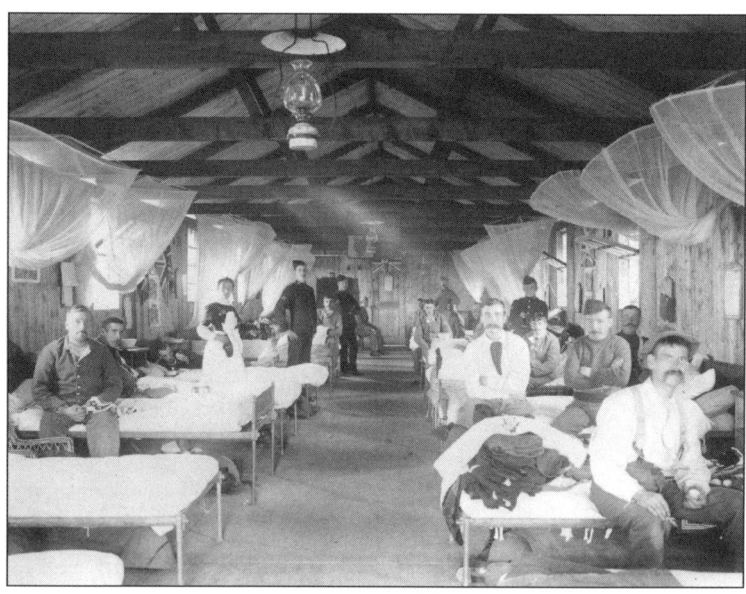

12: A typical hospital ward. Like many who served in South Africa, Adamson was hospitalized (in November 1900) after contracting enteric fever.

13: Soldiers of 4 CMR and 6 CMR departing Halifax aboard the Winnifredian, May 1902. Adamson's second trip to South Africa would ultimately prove abortive as peace was declared later in the month.

14: Mounted Rifles in camp at Durban. Agar spent some time here before finally returning to Canada, never having the chance to fight the Boers again.

15: Lieutenant-Colonel Agar Adamson, Princess Patricia's Canadian Light Infantry. The experience that he gained during his time with Strathcona's Horse would serve him well during the First World War. His monocle eventually became the stuff of legend in the Canadian Corps.

16: Agar in his element. A mess dinner at Christmas (seated second from bottom on left).

Introduction

Learning occurs in any number of ways. From childhood to maturity, people continue to acquire knowledge by reading, by listening to others speak on a particular point, by passively observing the world around them, by actively inquiring into a definite matter and by drawing lessons from their own varied experiences. And certainly, not everyone learns in the same manner as others, nor does everyone prefer to learn in a group setting, however large or small. The methods to accrue wisdom are just as varied as knowledge itself.

Individuals, as well as larger organizations, frequently synthesize experience into practical lessons that can guide future conduct in the hope of both avoiding mistakes and replicating success.[1] Through the *In Harm's Way* series, the Canadian Forces Leadership Institute (CFLI) has committed itself to acquiring and publishing the past experiences of soldiers, sailors and air personnel, usually drawn from recent operations, in order that others might learn from their triumphs and, on occasion sadly, their failures. While the present volume is not part of this broader series *per se*, its intent and purpose are remarkably similar.[2] Short leadership profiles such as this:

> ... represent a wealth of information that can help others to prepare for operations and leadership in general. They provide challenges and possible solutions that can be used by those who find themselves in similar circumstances. In essence, they can act as virtual experience for those who have not had the opportunity to deploy on operations either in Canada or overseas.[3]

In the words of noted military historian Sir John Keegan, "History, too, can be pressed into the service of familiarizing the young officer [or young recruit] with the unknown."[4]

And now the natural question arises: what knowledge can a lieutenant from a society that differs in so many important respects from our own and who fought in a conflict some 100 years ago possibly impart about leadership in the new, complex and ever changing security environment? This volume is very much an attempt to learn from past experience, for many of the leadership challenges faced in earlier years are just the same as they are today. Truly, "There are many situations, problems and dilemmas that are timeless and transcend missions or geographic areas."[5] Leaders of all generations have, for instance, always wondered how best to motivate their subordinates, how best to maintain discipline, how best to deal with their own personal fear and apprehensions, and most importantly, how best to lead in a manner that accomplishes the mission while expending life and limb appropriately. Usually they find the right answer, but in some cases they do not. Either way, their experiences can inform, guide and direct those who follow. While the context in which such lessons are offered in this volume is certainly dated – some might argue however that the British campaign in South Africa against an enemy that blended easily with the local population, used unconventional tactics and possessed minimal resources is akin to those situations now being faced in Afghanistan and Iraq – the lessons themselves are still relevant and will surely be of value to current members of the profession of arms, whether in garrison or whilst deployed. To be sure, describing those situations that our military predecessors faced provides experiential and vicarious knowledge that may prove exceedingly useful. This is not to say that Agar Adamson was right in everything that he did, for undoubtedly he was not. Rather, some *possible* avenues of action are suggested in passing that *might* be followed should similar situations arise in the future.

Hopefully the following pages will also offer a good story! This short volume serves to further address the dearth of literature that explores the individual accomplishments of Canadian soldiers during the South African War.[6] Senior officers have received the majority of scholarly attention over the years, much to the detriment of those who soldiered in less-lofty, but nonetheless important positions, such as the captains and lieutenants, the sergeants and corporals, upon whom much of the burden of leading at the "pointiest end of the sharp end" invariably fell. Aside from a now-waning desire to study only the "Great Men," these historiographic lapses have partially resulted from the fact that those in senior positions tend to be better documented than their subordinates by virtue of their position, responsibilities and accomplishments. The availability of such records has thus limited what truly can be known about the life and experiences of certain lower-placed individuals.

History is indeed fortunate to be able to claim Agar Adamson, for his life during the South African War, whether in Canada, in England or elsewhere, is extremely well documented. The completeness of the historical record is truly outstanding, for as a lieutenant in Strathcona's Horse (SH), many of his successes and his failures, his fears and his joys, are extremely well preserved. We could only be so lucky if all of the nation's military leaders, both junior and senior alike, were as well represented. His personal and intimate correspondence with his wife, in which he endeavoured to keep her informed of his campaign progress and, at times, confessed his feelings about his soldiers and questioned his own abilities, represents a significant repository of source material and has been cited extensively herein. As a romantic trapped in the late-Victorian and early-Edwardian eras, his letters are full of love for a woman who became his closest confidant and friend. His candid and frank admissions to her are surely not complete, nor are they entirely accurate on some scores – there were probably certain details in his writing that he purposely omitted or embellished – but these documents offer profound insight into his development as a leader over the course of the war. His transformation from a part-time militia enthusiast who lacked any meaningful experience with command into a competent, self-assured and effective officer can easily be observed in his private correspondence. Were it not for his prolific letters, any analysis of his career would be based largely on official records and on the writing of those soldiers who served under him, and while both sources are valuable, neither can provide the depth necessary to truly understand Agar as a private individual and as a soldier. Some readers may take issue with the heavy reliance on his correspondence with his wife, for it is possible that Agar may have attempted at times to portray himself as the hero and to exaggerate at the expense of truth. Although this criticism is valid enough, allowing the man to speak for himself permits his character to be more fully understood and appreciated than would otherwise have been possible through historical interpretation alone; where possible, his comments are balanced against those of others in an attempt to arrive at a more accurate depiction of events.

The numerous diaries, letters and memoirs created by many of the men who served under Adamson at various times throughout his South African career likewise record his character, personality and style of leadership. Given the relatively small number of soldiers for whom he was frequently responsible, 50 or so at most, the existence of so many documents of this sort is indeed astounding and highly fortunate. Is it simply coincidence that the soldiers of SH saw fit to record their impressions of Agar in the course of their daily musings, or did he so impress them with his charisma and affability, or conversely, his lack of ability, that they felt somehow obligated to comment? Taken together, such "personal writings," whether from Agar himself or his men, vividly illustrate the growth of a relatively young idealistic officer into a competent leader who met with considerable success on the battlefield. All in all, he is probably one of the best-documented junior officers of the late-nineteenth and early-twentieth centuries, although, as will become apparent, his background, personal connections and lifestyle make him somewhat atypical and not entirely representative of others from his generation. Faced with an abundance of material, therefore, Agar Adamson seemed a worthy candidate to analyze in order to further understand the nuances of leadership at some of the lowest levels of command.

The completeness of the historical record was certainly not the only reason that prompted an investigation of Adamson's life at the turn-of-the-century. This brief study also offers insight into how exactly Canada's second Victoria Cross (VC) of the South African War was won.[7] By their very nature, citations for such awards describe the action(s) being acknowledged, but rarely explain how the situation came to be that compelled the individual in question to act; background details are often, and understandably, omitted. Why was soldier X forced to discharge his duty in such a gallant manner? Was it superior enemy dispositions? Incompetence on the part of his leaders? Unforeseen circumstances? Analyzing the engagement at Wolve Spruit in which Sergeant A.H.L. Richardson of SH earned his VC will hopefully shed additional light on his personal valour in the face of overwhelming odds and, of more significance to the present volume, on Adamson's leadership during this brief engagement.

And finally, his accomplishments during the First World War are, to be sure, more widely known than his endeavours during the South African War some 15 years earlier. In the autumn of 1914, he returned to active military service as a captain with the Princess Patricia's Canadian Light Infantry (PPCLI). Over the next three years, he would earn the Distinguished Service Order (DSO) as a major,[8] would eventually be promoted to lieutenant-colonel, would assume temporary command of the 7th Brigade of the Canadian Corps in which the PPCLI fought, and would lead his troops, whether at the company- or battalion-level, through many costly and bloody battles. His story is truly remarkable, being an "original" that served continuously in one capacity or another from start to finish. Even a passing glance at his extensive correspondence during this period, again with his beloved Mabel, reveals that he employed many of the same leadership techniques that he either relied upon or refined whilst serving on the veldt in South Africa.[9] Unfortunately, his later military career is beyond the scope of this brief discussion – such a study would surely prove extremely interesting – although it seems reasonable to suggest that his earlier experiences played a significant role in defining the leader that would come to such prominence during the war in France and Belgium.[10] If such is true, his later successes cannot be completely understood and appreciated without some reference to his formative years. Agar was not static in his outlook, but rather changed as his career, experience and knowledge broadened. Certain lessons he undoubtedly learned in the muddy trenches, but the foundation that influenced his leadership style and abilities was apparently formed at a much earlier stage and these initial lessons held a certain amount of sway over how he carried himself throughout his entire military career. Of course, these assumptions remain exactly that without a complete examination of his personal story during the First World War, but this volume represents a starting point for those so interested in understanding Adamson as a soldier.

This volume, first and foremost, attempts to identify both the positives and negatives of Agar's leadership and to illustrate how the former eventually came to outnumber the latter. While he was successful in many of his undertakings, he failed in others and these setbacks were sometimes costly in terms of casualties. Because his military career provides the compass by which this volume is directed, Adamson occasionally appears unidimensional and monochromatic in the pages that follow; truly, though, he was a man possessed of personality, wit, honour and charm, with the traditional biases and obligations of his day. Other historians have offered their interpretations of his personal life and have gained considerable access to his inner character simply by the subjects that they have studied. In much the same manner, this book seeks to gain access to his military character by virtue of the experiences that are examined. Taken together, however, this body of literature offers an interesting perspective on the whole Adamson.[11]

C.L.M.
Kingston

Endnotes

1   During the First World War for instance, the Canadian Corps, the overseas component of the Canadian Expeditionary Force that fought in France and Belgium, engaged in an after-action review process whereby the factors that contributed to successes and failures during the last battle were identified and forwarded to higher command for consideration. If such opinions held merit, elements of certain tactical and operational doctrines

might then have been changed or maintained as is in order to replicate the positives and to avoid failure. See Bill Rawling, *Surviving Trench Warfare: Technology and the Canadian Corps, 1914-1918* (Toronto: University of Toronto Press, 1992) and Shane Schreiber, *Shock Army of the British Empire: The Canadian Corps in the Last 100 Days of the Great War* (Westport: Praeger, 1997).

2   The *In Harm's Way* series is only one component of the much larger Strategic Leadership Writing Project that, by creating a distinct body of Canadian leadership knowledge, endeavours to assist with the professional development of military personnel, as well as to educate the public in regards to the Canadian Forces' contributions to the nation. The first volume in this set, which is cited below in note 3, has recently been joined by another. See Colonel Bernd Horn, ed., *In Harm's Way – Serving the Greater Good: Perspectives of Operational Duty* (Kingston: CDA Press, 2006).

3   Major-General Paul Hussey, Commander, Canadian Defence Academy (CDA), in Foreword to Colonel Bernd Horn, ed., *In Harm's Way – On the Front Lines of Leadership: Sub-Unit Command on Operations* (Kingston: CDA Press, 2006), iii.

4   Sir John Keegan, *The Face of Battle: A Study of Agincourt, Waterloo and the Somme* (London: Pimlico, 2004), 22.

5   Colonel Bernd Horn in Introduction to Horn, *Sub-Unit Command on Operations*, v.

6   The literature that examines the careers of certain Canadian officers includes: Desmond Morton, *The Canadian General: Sir William Otter* (Toronto: Hakkert, 1974); John Macfarlane, "The Right Stuff? Evaluating the Performance of Lieutenant-Colonel F.-L Lessard in South Africa and his Failure to Receive a Senior Command Position with the CEF in 1914," *Canadian Military History* 8, 3 (1999), 48-58; Ronald Haycock: *Sam Hughes: The Public Career of a Controversial Canadian, 1885-1916* (Waterloo: Wilfrid Laurier University Press, 1986); and more generally, Carman Miller, *Painting the Map Red: Canada and the South African War, 1899-1902* (Montreal & Kingston: McGill-Queen's University Press, 1993).

7   Richardson was the second Canadian to win the VC during the South African War, the first being W.H.S. Nickerson of the Royal Army Medical Corps., who was born in New Brunswick in 1875. Richardson was the first member of a Canadian unit to earn this coveted decoration.

8   See David K. Riddle and Donald G. Mitchell, *The Distinguished*

Service Order to the Canadian Expeditionary Force and Canadians in the Royal Naval Air Service, Royal Flying Corps and Royal Air Force, 1915-1920 (Winnipeg: The Kirkby-Marlton Press, 1991), 1. See also, *London Gazette*, 3 Jun 1916, and, *Canada Gazette*, 1 Jul 1916. Because Adamson's DSO was awarded on the occasion of His Majesty's birthday in 1916, no citation is available that describes the reason for the award, unlike for those that were given in recognition of a specific act. Such awards, however, were oftentimes offered in recognition of continued exemplary performance.

9   Adamson's current popularity may have much to do with the recent publication of his First World War letters. See Agar Adamson, Norm Christie, ed., *The Letters of Agar Adamson, 1914-1919* (Nepean: CEF Books, 1997). The original copies of these letters are preserved in the Agar Stewart Allan Masterton Adamson fonds, Manuscript Group 30 – E149, *Library and Archives Canada*.

10   Those desiring to examine Adamson's First World War career may wish to begin with the following resources, which by no means form a comprehensive bibliography: David Jay Bercuson, *The Patricias: The Proud History of the Princess Patricia's Canadian Light Infantry, 1914-1920* (Toronto: Stoddart Publishing, 2001); Lieutenant-Colonel Ian McCulloch, "Crisis in Leadership: The Seventh Brigade & the Nivelles 'Mutiny', 1918," *Army Doctrine and Training Bulletin* 3, 2 (Summer 2000), 35-46; Sandra Gwyn, *Tapestry of War: A Private View of Canadians in the Great War* (Toronto: HarperCollins, 1992); Patrick H. Brennan, "Good Men for a Hard Job: Infantry Battalion Commanders in the Canadian Expeditionary Force," *The Canadian Army Journal*, 9.1 (Spring 2006), 9-28; Ralph Hodder-Williams, *Princess Patricia's Canadian Light Infantry* (London: Hodder and Stoughton, 1923); and, Jeffery Williams, *First in the Field: Gault of the Patricias* (London: L. Cooper, 1995).

11   For a good study of Adamson's character, in which his military exploits are explored to some degree, see Sandra Gwyn, *The Private Capital: Ambition and Love in the Age of Macdonald and Laurier* (Toronto: McClelland & Stewart, 1984), especially chapter 24, 343-370.

Learning the Hard Way

This war is, however, a valuable experience to every one.[1]

In a letter home immediately before the impending Canadian attack at Vimy in the spring of 1917, Lieutenant-Colonel A.S.A.M. Adamson, the Commanding Officer (CO) of the Princess Patricia's Canadian Light Infantry (PPCLI), bitterly complained to his wife:

> Every man in England wants a commission. I get about 15 letters a day. ... I am afraid my answers to these wretches will not please them. Fathers write me, M.P.s [Members of Parliament] write me and Mothers and Sisters, and in nearly every case the men are not worth considering and I cannot help telling them that the men out here who have stuck it and are sticking it, are the only ones I can consider. The Corps Commander [Sir Julian Byng] has allowed me to send in the names of 20 N.C.O.s [Non-Commissioned Officers] and men for commissions, which looks as if he expected we would need them fairly soon. It has been quite difficult to pick them out as sahibs won't go round and there are more important factors to consider than Mess and table manners in this serious Push. The power of leadership, which I think is born rather than acquired, I consider first. After that, quick decision and, even in training, quick action and the ability to realize the situation he finds himself in.[2]

After serving continuously since 1914 and having witnessed firsthand the slaughter that became so endemic of the Western

Front, Adamson was convinced that promotion in the field should be based on merit and ability and not, as had earlier been the case, on overt patronage and political connection.[3] Being responsible for the overall effectiveness of his regiment and being ever aware of the value of life, he was loath to place the welfare of his soldiers in the hands of untested and inexperienced leaders, especially when knowledgeable men were already serving in the ranks, many of whom possessed command experience as NCOs.[4] Politics and patronage would not be pandered to under his leadership, much to the chagrin of certain socially ambitious citizens.[5]

Yet, ironically, nearly two decades earlier during the opening days of the South African War, Adamson himself was exactly the type of man he would later come to describe as "wretched." Ambitious, extremely well-connected, eager to serve and possessing little real military experience, he relied heavily on his own political and social affiliations, and even on those of his powerful and wealthy wife, to secure a commission that would take him to the sun and sand of South Africa. Aided in no small measure by an impressive retinue of influential patrons, Adamson's persistence and determination were eventually rewarded with a lieutenant's commission in Strathcona's Horse (SH), a regiment raised for imperial service by Donald Smith, more familiarly known as Lord Strathcona, the Canadian High Commissioner in London.[6]

Born in 1865 on Christmas day in Montreal, Agar Stewart Allan Masterson Adamson came from a distinguished family that possessed a long and notable association with public service. His father, James, oftentimes served as clerk to the Senate of Canada, while his paternal grandfather, William Agar, who styled himself a Doctor of Divinity, was chaplain to both the senate and to Her Majesty's forces in the Canadas. His mother, Mary Julia, was the daughter of Stewart Derbishire, printer to the crown. Living a life of privilege, Agar received a private education at Trinity College in Port Hope, Ontario, and later travelled to England to read for the holy orders at Corpus Christi, Cambridge. A gifted athlete and rider, he rowed and played field sports at university and once rode his own horse to victory in the Newmarket stakes. He returned to Ottawa in 1890 after deciding not to enter the ministry and joined the civil service where he served the senate like his father.[7]

After connecting himself with the government of the land, he embarked upon a military career that would ultimately prove to be an adventurous and defining period in his life. The time that he spent under arms and his experience of war would transform him from an innocent to a veteran and would bring him to the realization that while patronage might have served the peacetime militia well, it certainly did not suffice in a professional army. In 1893, he was commissioned as a second-lieutenant in Number 4 Company of the Governor General's Foot Guards (GGFG) and, by 1899, had been promoted to captain. A host of ceremonial duties marking such events as state dinners, the opening and closing of various sessions of parliament, the departure of the Governor General from Ottawa and, more specifically, the unveiling of a monument to Sir John A. Macdonald, Canada's first Prime Minister, provided much of his early military experience, experience that was largely decorative in nature and of little practical value.[8]

Perhaps owing to his many and varied connections, which his social, political and military positions allowed him to cultivate, he once served on the staff of Major-General E.T.H. Hutton, the General Officer Commanding the Canadian Militia, at the "autumn manoeuvres."[9] Interestingly, Adamson was a friend of Lord Minto, the Governor General at the close of the nineteenth century, and Minto, in turn, was a "close personal friend" of Hutton.[10] His acquaintances included other Governors General as well, for he was a friend of Lord Dufferin's son, Lord Ava.[11] Adamson's rank and connections seem to have assured him a place at a Staff Ride that was held in Niagara in May 1899.[12] His associations, whether expanded by his own affable personality or derived from his father's and grandfather's years of service to the Crown, granted him access to the political and military élite of his day, a privileged position that he exploited to the absolute fullest.

Being a product of the late-nineteenth century Canadian militia, however, he possessed little real command experience. Leading soldiers through the rote and predictable movements of a ceremonial parade could certainly not be equated with leading tired, hungry and frightened soldiers against a stubborn enemy. For him, as for many of his contemporaries, the militia was more of a social diversion, a gentleman's club, which could be used to supplement one's income, however modestly, and to add an element of prestige and pedigree to one's social resume. Truly, "In a society acutely conscious of social status, a militia commission became a badge of social respectability."[13] Even the annual camps that Adamson attended probably offered little in the way of practical experience that could be put to good use as much of the training was "simple and repetitious" and consisted primarily of drills, some range work and a sham battle.[14] In many respects, he was typical of his fellow soldiers who likewise harboured military ambitions since he exemplified the "the Protestant, middle-class character of the pre-war militia's officer ranks," although his extensive connections certainly distinguished him from others.[15]

In November 1899, only weeks after the outbreak of war, Agar married Ann Mabel Cawthra, the only daughter of successful businessman John Cawthra.[16] Held at St. George's Church in Toronto, their nuptials were described by one local newspaper as "the chief of the fashionable fall weddings."[17] True to his adventurous nature, he honeymooned with his new bride in Mexico on horseback. Although Adamson married into high society, he was not totally unfamiliar with such circles given his upbringing, past endeavours and present position. In fact, he felt quite at ease in such genteel and refined surroundings and was truly in his element.[18] Like all marriages at times, they endured difficult periods over the next couple of years, especially when Agar placed his military ambitions above all else.

Halifax

Despite being recently married, Agar soon travelled to Halifax where, until April 1900, he served with the 3rd (Special Service) Battalion, Royal Canadian Regiment of Infantry (RCRI), a hastily recruited unit that allowed the Leinster Regiment, the regular British garrison at Wellington Barracks, to be released for service elsewhere in the empire.[19] His time in Nova Scotia's capital, although brief, afforded Agar an opportunity to not only refine, but to develop further, his particular style of leadership. Full-time service, as opposed to the one-night-a-week routine that he had been accustomed to, was indeed a welcome change for it brought him closer to realizing his ambition of serving in South Africa. In one of his first surviving letters home, he described for Mabel some of his less pleasing, but nonetheless interesting, responsibilities:

> Our duty being to parade the low parts of the town from 8 to 10 to gather in all drunken men and search all houses of ill fame, which is done by entering them in the Queen[']s name back and front, and searching for men,

the officer remaining outside. The low part of the town like all garrison and seaport towns is very low. The duty is not a pleasant one and comes round every 16 days. We found men both drunk and otherwise and march[ed] them to the guard room & this morning they received their punishments.[20]

Aside from offering a vivid social commentary on turn-of-the-century Halifax, Adamson's remarks to his wife reveal that he was more than prepared to enforce discipline when required and was resolute in ensuring that his subordinates followed the rules and regulations of the service, an attitude that he continued to hold dear during the months and years that followed.

Agar's duties in Halifax were largely confined to those typical of a garrison setting. Having spent a good deal of time with the GGFG, he probably did not find his service in the provisional battalion to be that much different from that which he had experienced in Ottawa, although there were certainly some initial challenges. Being authorized and raised in the span of a few short weeks, the battalion experienced a number of early difficulties that tested the resolve and ability of officers and men alike. Amongst others, recruiting shortages, insufficient rations, a spate of illnesses and the ensuing dissatisfaction of a large number of soldiers after certain parts of the city were placed out of bounds (and for good reason!), all combined to place significant demands on the battalion's leadership.[21] Simply dealing with such difficulties, while at the same time maintaining some semblance of order and morale, must have been a daunting task for all concerned. Despite these problems, however, the battalion's CO, Lieutenant-Colonel Vidal, vainly reassured the Militia Department, "Everything working smoothly and regiment getting nicely into shape."[22] He could not have been further from the truth.

As if the difficulties internal to the battalion were not quite enough, the *Canadian Military Gazette* criticized the appointment of certain officers to the Halifax garrison. The journal wondered, "Were the best officers available appointed to positions?" and concluded "that in many instances seniority and worth have been made secondary to personal and political influence." Aside from considering the majority of appointments to be poor, the *Gazette* took grave exception with the fact that certain officers "are known among the militia as being incapable and useless; and at least one is a newly joined subaltern who, we understand, has never seen a day's soldiering in his life."[23] Criticism of the battalion also came from within. Writing under the pseudonym, "A Private in the Rear Ranks," one disgruntled soldier stressed that "we are not properly used down here in Halifax. Our officers are a little 'on the pig,' and don't care for their men as they ought." All in all, he considered his officers to be "no good."[24]

Outside of his regular duties, however, other opportunities for Adamson to further develop his practical leadership skills soon arose. As he related to Mabel, he was:

> ...given charge of 35 men as a fire brigade for one month. It has to be organized and in a few days the General will send up a staff officer to ring the fire alarm and will make his report accordingly. I am on duty till 1 o'clock tonight. I think I shall ring the alarm after that for practice.[25]

His comments, while brief and passing, reveal that he took to his responsibilities with some interest, vigour and concern. By taking the initiative, challenging his men and offering them realistic training, he sought to increase their efficiency and to develop them into a cohesive team that could perform competently. Rather than waiting to see how they would react during an actual fire, or during an evaluated exercise upon which their (and his) reputation would hang, he attempted to prepare his soldiers-cum-firefighters with additional practices and to ensure that they at least knew the rudiments of their responsibilities. A proactive training regime, he believed, might save him from later exercises to correct deficiencies in the brigade's performance. Whether they appreciated being woken at such an early hour to respond to imaginary flames is doubtful.

Unfortunately, Adamson's personal and intimate correspondence with his wife – she truly became his closest friend and confidant – does not reveal more about his military duties in Halifax. He nevertheless seems to have had some opportunity to exercise a degree of command and to refine his leadership skills that had been seeded during his early years of militia service. When not occupied with his military duties though, Agar spent a considerable amount of time trying to establish a life for Mabel and himself in the city. Much energy and ink were expended on finding suitable accommodation in Halifax and worrying about those things that only the privileged do: servants; cooks; parties; dining at Government House; and membership in the local golf club. In these respects, Agar was simply attempting to continue the lifestyle to which he and Mabel were accustomed. His attempts to situate himself in the local gentry certainly paralleled those of the other officers of the garrison, especially his British predecessors, who "enhanced the genteel tone of the urban élite," while at the same time, "the enlisted men contributed to the drunkenness and destitution of underclass Halifax."[26]

Despite the fierce criticism levelled against the officers of the garrison, his superiors and subordinates alike held Adamson in high regard. Upon his departure from the city to assume his duties with Strathcona's Horse, one Halifax newspaper recorded:

> Captain Adamson was one of the most efficient officers in the regiment. He acted as lieutenant of D company, and was extremely popular with officers and men. ... Before the train left Captain Adamson addressed the men, thanking them for their kindly wishes and assuring them of his deep interest in their welfare. ... Three hearty cheers were given for Captain Adamson as the train pulled out from the station.[27]

If such a report can be believed, Agar was apparently one of the better officers of the regiment. The disparaging comments made against his peers did not necessarily apply to him in their entirety, if at all. In the end, his time in the city provided further opportunities to gain experience in exercising command and in being responsible for the good conduct, welfare and competence of those beneath him, all lessons that would indeed serve him well in the months that followed. Just how he came to be selected for service in South Africa reveals much about Agar's character, personality and standing in turn-of-the-century Ottawa, not to mention how significant a role patronage played in the militia of the day.

Strathcona's Horse

In January 1900, Lord Strathcona began planning in earnest for "my little Force for South Africa." His contribution to the empire's efforts was to consist of:

> ...400 mounted men, to be recruited chiefly from Manitoba, the North-West Territories, and British Columbia, to be composed indifferently of English or French-speaking Canadians. The Force to consist of unmarried men as far as possible, all of whom are to be

expert marksmen, at home in the saddle, and thoroughly efficient to act as rough-riders or scouts.[28]

In addition, Strathcona desired that "the Force to be raised should be thoroughly efficient in every way, that the men and the officers should be the most suitable that can be obtained for the services for which they are likely to be required."[29] His soldiers were duly recruited and eventually concentrated in Ottawa for a brief period to draw stores and to begin their training, all of which was conducted under the supervision of their new CO, Lieutenant-Colonel Sam Steele, formerly of the North-West Mounted Police (NWMP).[30] Imbibing a motley collection of volunteers with a proper military bearing proved difficult since "Many of the men were enthusiastic for service, but not tempered as soldiers."[31] Queen Victoria's newest recruits did not have long to wait for their adventure to begin, for they soon left for South Africa after a relatively short stay in the city.

A mere one month later, Strathcona received word from the British War Office (WO) that he should, if feasible, raise a small draft of soldiers that could eventually replace casualties in the regiment proper.[32] The WO feared that reductions in strength, whether caused by Boer bullets or disease, would impair the unit's fighting effectiveness and so it was intended that this reserve of men would be used to keep the force at full strength.[33] Wasting little time, Strathcona sought to enlist the same type of men and in generally the same area from which the main body had been drawn. Writing to the Minister of Militia and Defence, Dr. Frederick William Borden,[34] he stressed that the "draft should be recruited Northwest as before."[35] Inspector Strickland of the NWMP was chosen to command the draft and to convey it to South Africa. Although apparently an ideal choice – a western rough-rider with much experience in handling both men and horses – Strathcona had a few concerns about his suitability as he was told that he was a "large heavy man and perhaps hardly suited for light cavalry work."[36] His fears were adequately reassured when he received word that the inspector "is the most suitable man available. He is a big man but athletic. Several of [the] first lot of officers were well over two hundred pounds."[37] Putting such concerns aside, Strathcona seemed pleased with this choice.

Contrary to expectations, though, Strickland declined the opportunity to command the draft. In fact, he "prefers not going" and expressed a clear "unwillingness to go."[38] In spite of his refusal to accompany the reinforcements overseas and to subsequently assume a position within the regiment proper, he spent the latter weeks of March and the early weeks of April recruiting the men who would fill the ranks of the draft. After coming down from the Yukon, he started selecting men in British Columbia, primarily in Vancouver and Revelstoke, and continued to add to his number in Calgary and Winnipeg as he made his way eastward toward Ottawa where the draft would be assembled and readied.[39] Since many in these towns and hinterlands probably knew him through his service with the NWMP, he surely relied on his stature and familiarity to attract recruits, especially since "Only men from the West will be taken, though numerous applications are pouring into the department from the eastern provinces."[40] Enthusiasm for the draft was evidently quite high in many of the centres that he visited for Strickland believed, perhaps somewhat optimistically, that "'Five hundred men could be as easily secured as fifty.'" Having so many volunteers from which to choose, he brought to Ottawa only "the pick of those who offered, and they are a trim and ready-looking lot of soldiers."[41]

Faced with Strickland's refusal, Strathcona was compelled to find a hasty replacement to command the draft. As before, aspirants from all points across Canada submitted an application for employment.[42] One individual, however, stood out from all others. Perhaps it was the well-placed patrons who offered their support for Adamson that caught Strathcona's eye. Agar's wife, Mabel, sent the first volley by telegram:

> YOU MAY REMEMBER ME AS MISS CAWTHRA YOUR GUEST GLENCOE AM NOW MARRIED TO CAPTAIN AGAR ADAMSON ACTIVE MILITIA MY HUSBAND MOST ANXIOUS TO TAKE CHARGE DRAFT STRATHCONA HORSE REFERENCE LORD MINTO HAS NECESSARY QUALIFICATIONS.[43]

Although Strathcona did not know him personally, any worries that he might have had were immediately put to rest when he received two additional telegrams that confirmed Adamson's suitability.[44] Borden thought Agar was a "good officer horseman and shot."[45] In much the same manner, Lord Minto opined: "I venture to recommend to you Capt Adamson, a friend of mine. Very anxious to join your Corps. Excellent officer & good rider."[46] Few other applicants could have boasted of such support and influence. After this flurry of telegraphic communication, Strathcona took little time to decide and immediately wired Borden that Adamson's nomination was indeed approved but that "he must go as [a] Lieutenant."[47] Although currently a captain, the WO was "asking only for officer [of] that rank."[48] Being anxious to serve, Adamson surely accepted this offer without much hesitation after considering both the "grave responsibility"[49] of leading untested soldiers against the enemy and the genuine opportunity to remove himself from "the dreary inanities of the Senate."[50] Whether or not he was somewhat dismayed at the accompanying reduction in rank, and thus in prestige and influence, is unknown. For him, the chance to expand his military horizons probably outweighed such meagre considerations; what he lacked in official rank could easily be made good through a reliance on his charm and wit when interacting with his superiors, whether British or Canadian. As events would prove, his time with the Strathconas would test both his abilities as a leader and his qualities as an officer, searching examinations that he was not entirely prepared for.

Ottawa, London and beyond

While Agar was busily endeavouring to secure a commission, the men of the SH draft arrived in Ottawa on the afternoon of 25 April 1900. Occasioning a good deal of excitement in the city, one local newspaper soon suggested that the draft's presence was nothing short of invigorating: "The men with the stetson hat and the wooly western ways are again in the city, and the military fervor that was beginning to die out has been given a fresh start."[51] Once assembled on the platform, the men were immediately taken from the train station to their quarters at Lansdowne Park where they were to be "clothed and equipped and held in readiness"[52] until their departure overseas.

After only a few days in Ottawa, however, a devastating fire scorched large sections of the city and the would-be soldiers were pressed into service as temporary firemen.[53] Although in no way trained for such work, "The men of the detachment did valient [sic] work at the fire on Thursday night. They were ... handed over to Chief Powell under whose direction they worked. Captain Adamson considers that they worked hard."[54] The experience that Agar had accrued in Halifax whilst in charge of the garrison's fire brigade was indeed put to good use on this unfortunate occasion. Incidentally, his praise for his soldiers, with whom he "soon became very popular" in the eyes of one of the draft's members, was not just confined to their firefighting abilities alone.[55] In fact, he "considered the men of the detachment especially good, and all were riders of experience. He has three of the best bronco hustlers in the west with him, and all the men are physically of the finest."[56]

Once the last smouldering embers had been extinguished and the citizens of Ottawa began to recover from the devastation wrought by the fire, assisted in part by the numerous donations that poured into the city from many points across Canada and abroad, the draft left Lansdowne Park for Montreal.[57] Much to their satisfaction and amusement, a large crowd of townsfolk and prominent militia officers met Adamson and the draft at the station on 30 April and "As the train pulled out the men were given three hearty cheers and wished God speed on their journey."[58] Inspector Strickland, who had recruited the would-be troopers and brought them to Ottawa, did not leave empty-handed for he departed the city on the same day with 42 new recruits for the NWMP, most of whom enlisted in the maritime provinces.[59] The train carrying the newest members of Strathcona's Horse rolled into Montreal in the evening, only a few hours after it had left Ottawa. The men were marched immediately from the Canadian Pacific Railway station to the docks where they boarded the Dominion liner *Vancouver* before nightfall. Having "presented a smart soldierly appearance as they marched through the streets," all were tendered an informal dinner and reception once onboard.[60] With the coming of the morning sun on 1 May, the draft exited the harbour, bound for England and eventually the seat of war.

Despite looking smart and neat,[61] the men of the draft were soldiers in name only. Of those who had left the familiar air of Canada to assist the empire in South Africa, only a handful, six

at most, possessed some form of previous military experience.⁶²
To compound matters even further, their time had not been spent constructively in training while in Ottawa, but rather in fighting fires and drawing their equipment from military stores. Most certainly, these men had left the city exactly as they had entered it, inexperienced, although they were now somewhat better dressed! Because Adamson did not recruit the draft himself – rather, he was placed in command once they had been mustered in the nation's capital – he would have to wait for a more appropriate time to begin building the familiarity, loyalty and trust that would contribute to their overall effectiveness and efficiency. With little or no meaningful opportunities for training or making acquaintances, Agar, who was now expected to properly lead his soldiers through whatever situations occured, was forced to play "catch-up" on both accounts while travelling to the front. Had he been able to select the men himself, this process could have at least commenced earlier, although fighting the fire in Ottawa together probably started to mould the draft, Adamson included, into a cohesive whole. More work certainly had to be done *en route*.

The trans-Atlantic crossing (from Canada to England) was calm and generally without significant incident, although Agar became quite sick halfway through the voyage.⁶³ He later recounted the particulars of the transit for the benefit and education of Lord Strathcona. Much to his own satisfaction, he wrote, "It is worth noting that they were enlisted, transported 2,000 miles, equipped and embarked for England in the very short span of 13 days," thus indicating that the soldiers had received little practical training. In an attempt to compensate for this marked lack of instruction, Adamson endeavoured to educate his men in the rudiments of soldiering whilst aboard ship. He recalled in the same letter, "The draft was drilled three hours a day, one hour before breakfast at physical drill, the remainder was such movements as where [sic] possible."⁶⁴ Being confined to the available deck space, such training was simple in its evolutions. Adamson could at least take comfort in the fact that they were now on their way to becoming soldiers in both name *and* ability. On the final day of the voyage to England, the men played sports and also had a concert, the proceeds of which, about $40, were to be given to "some patriotic fund."⁶⁵

According to David Morrison Stewart, one of the soldiers recruited for the draft, Adamson also used this time to give "us a very nice lecture on how to carry ourselves and what we would likely have to go through."⁶⁶ During this discussion, he surely set forth his expectations and conveyed the message, whether explicitly or implicitly, that they were not to tarnish the good name of the regiment (and thus their benefactor) with which they now had the privilege of being associated. Judging by their later conduct, however, some of the soldiers misinterpreted Adamson's plea to act like gentlemen. How much practical military advice he could offer to his would-be soldiers is questionable given that his experience extended only so far as the Canadian militia in Ottawa and the minimal time that he had spent in attempting to assemble a competent garrison in Halifax. Lacking wartime service, and thus the credibility that derived from it, his advice probably consisted of relevant anecdotes and a few interesting stories that he thought were applicable at the time. Not having fought in any previous conflict, his counsel was surely limited in value, but at least he attempted to inform his soldiers to the best of his knowledge and ability. Depending on the content of his lecture and the degree to which he was believable, his men may have taken some comfort from the fact that their officer at least appeared to be knowledgeable in "things military." For their part, he knew more than they did and that was probably good enough … for now.

The *Vancouver* reached the shores of England on 10 May and docked at Liverpool. Being on a tight schedule, the draft could not enjoy the city, but rather left for the Royal Albert Docks in London soon after their arrival. Meeting his reinforcements immediately before their departure for South Africa on 11 May aboard the British transport *Assaye*, Lord Strathcona, accompanied by a large and enthusiastic crowd, "bade them God-speed" and expressed his "belief that they would emulate the excellent example of the other Canadians at the front." Soon thereafter, "the men cheered the High Commissioner most vociferously" once he had finished inspecting his soldiers, all of whom "were in good form and excellent spirits."[67] The *Assaye*, which included drafts for other regiments now at the front,[68] soon exited the harbour bound for South Africa.

Unlike the trip to England, this voyage was somewhat more eventful. As with all long transits, the soldiers occupied themselves with a diversity of activities. An outbreak of scarlet fever unfortunately forced all to remain aboard ship when they reached St. Vincent for coaling. The soldiers thus amused themselves by tossing pennies into the crystalline waters for the "native boys" to dive for, although a death from a fall while coal was being loaded cast a shroud over such jovial amusements.[69] To keep fit, Adamson participated in an officers' boxing contest, during which he received a good deal of bodily punishment, but ultimately proved victorious. He also attended a dinner to celebrate a recent British victory and spent time making his acquaintance with "three most charming old Colonels [and] a sporting little steeplechasing Major," whom he undoubtedly regaled with his stories of his winning days at the Newmarket stakes.[70]

Despite his attempts to further his already-extensive list of connections, a habit that he seemed unwilling or unable to break,

Adamson still ensured that his troopers received training. Being concerned that his men lacked proficiency in certain military arts, which they truly did, he again endeavoured to impart certain skills. As he recalled in one of his letters home, he was most pleased that "They made very good shooting yesterday in spite of the rifle being quite new to them."[71] Like before, the men were "drilled daily including physical drill at 6 a.m."[72] Adamson was relieved when he found his men "keen to learn and not frightened of hard work."[73] His efforts seem to have paid in the end, for as he later related to Lord Strathcona, "many complimentary remarks have been made to me on their…general appearance and I am sure if they give us a chance you will have every reason to be proud of us."[74] Adamson and his soldiers would not have to wait long for an opportunity to test what they had learned and to reveal their true level of soldierly competence. How prepared they were for open warfare after a few weeks of training in the confined areas of the two ships remained to be seen.

South Africa

On 10 June, the *Assaye* finally reached South Africa.[75] Adamson and his men soon moved to Maitland Camp, a mere seven miles from Cape Town, where he found that "Most of the men and officers are half invalids from the front."[76] The main body of Strathconas had just left the encampment six days before, having been assigned the task of destroying an important bridge.[77] Being eager to see the front, Adamson became somewhat dejected when he was forced to wait since "I have no orders yet and no horses here for me, but hear they are somewhere."[78] Interestingly, on proceeding inland from the coast, David Stewart noted with some pride that they all had been "Treated to beer & cigars on the way to camp by the Captain."[79] Adamson's munificence on this occasion undoubtedly served as a reward for his men who had worked exceedingly hard on both legs of the voyage from Canada and who had not been able to enjoy the local establishments in Liverpool, London or St. Vincent. Given the tedium and restraints of shipboard life, these unexpected yet welcomed gifts surely aided morale, especially amongst the smokers and drinkers of the draft, of which there was probably no shortage of either.[80] Seeing that Agar was responsible for his soldiers' conduct, it is unlikely that he allowed them to drink to excess, but if he did, he surely removed himself before the effects of intoxication became apparent. A gentleman, to be sure, would never be seen participating in such activities with his men. On this occasion, he undoubtedly maintained his professional distance and never truly befriended his soldiers in order that he might remain impartial should he be called upon to enforce discipline, which he often did with vigour. That he was genuinely interested in their welfare is clear, but he never related to them as his equal, seeing that he was from an entirely different social and military class than they.

After being warned to be ready to move on short notice as a separate unit, Adamson kept himself and the draft busy by "drawing extra stores." As he recalled:

> We have all plenty of work to do and the men are kept at it most of the time, though no drill to speak of, but my darling Mabel, it is very lonely work with no other officer to help me and having to decide everything myself and act entirely on my own responsibility.

His comments reflect some of his frustration with the "red tape staff officers [who] don't give a damn for anybody and would look upon it as a capital joke to send you off only half outfitted."[81] Yet, they also suggest that Adamson was beginning to feel the pressure of command and that he might have been questioning his ability to lead at this point. Serving in an active theatre of operations, as opposed to the stately environments of either Ottawa or Halifax, seems to have presented Agar with a number of challenges that he was not entirely prepared for or equipped to deal with.[82] Along this line, one of his contemporaries once wrote, "There is no question that leadership in war is the most difficult and responsible position in which a man can be placed."[83] The change in his mood after arriving in South Africa, where his enthusiasm or lack of decisiveness could mean the difference between life and death, not only for himself but for his troopers as well, seems to have weighed heavily. Mistakes onboard ship or in Canada could largely be forgiven, but overseas, as he was now realizing, most certainly could not. The above sentiments also imply that Agar desired reassurance that he was acting appropriately and doing the right things. The absence of other officers who could validate his conduct, or correct it, coupled with the fact that he could not for professional reasons speak to his men about his own performance, lest they question his competence, became a source of stress. The loneliness of command had truly set in.

Before leaving camp, a number of changes in the composition of the draft further compounded his mounting problems. By leaving some men behind "with beastly diseases they caught from filthy women,"[84] while at the same time assuming command of others whom the main body of Strathconas had not taken along when it left the staging area, Adamson became saddled with a number of new soldiers whom he knew little about and, conversely, who knew little about him. The time involved in transporting the draft from Ottawa to Cape Town at least provided an opportunity for Agar to become acquainted with his soldiers and for them to become familiar with his particular style of leadership,

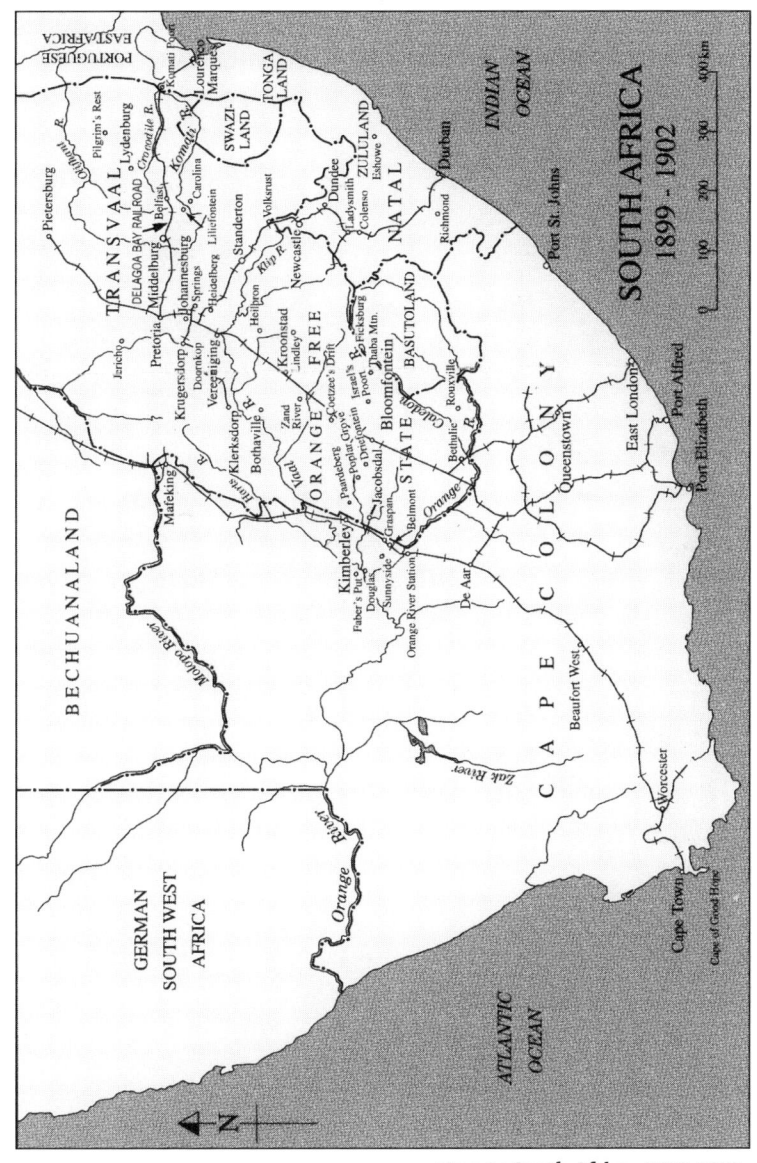

Map 1: South Africa, 1899-1902.

personality and expectations. This transfer of personnel partially upset some of his efforts and might have, in the end, contributed to the stress that Adamson seems to have been feeling. If he had felt any degree of comfort in his relations with his men owing to the time that they had spent together thus far, he must have likewise been dismayed at the prospect of starting all over again with his newest soldiers, especially since there were so many other pressing demands that were competing for his attention and effort. After realizing that some of his work had been for naught, and that a considerable amount still awaited him, Agar began to feel somewhat despondent and demoralized.

After completing their stay at Maitland, Adamson and his now-altered draft boarded the *Idaho* and left for Durban in Natal where they would begin their journey to join the main body of Strathconas who were now fighting with General Sir Redvers Buller's Natal Field Force.[85] Before they reached their final destination, however, the vessel called at Port Elizabeth and East London. As another member of the draft later recalled, "at the former place a party of us went ashore and excited some curiosity amongst the townspeople who had never before seen troops from far-away Canada."[86] Speaking of the same incident, yet another soldier recorded in his dairy:

> Cap't Adamson sticks up for his men in good shape. Was telling some of the boys that the people here had a very exaggerated account of our capabilities as horsemen and he didn't try to undeceive them so we were to do the best we can. Said they object to our saddles because they were too heavy but he said they were good enough for us. [87]

By relating to his men the details of his encounter with some of the local inhabitants, Adamson instilled them with a sense of pride by expressing his confidence and trust, even though he had had little opportunity to observe their martial abilities or their horsemanship. He apparently saw no reason to deflate a rumour that served the purposes of building morale. By actively encouraging the unfounded impressions held by the townsfolk, Adamson implied to those under his command that he expected them to meet the standard of conduct and performance that he had just set. Since he publicly expressed his faith in them, whatever his private opinions may have been, they undoubtedly felt obliged to demonstrate to their leader that his comments were indeed true, well founded and deserved. Most certainly, the "Cap't seems proud of his men."[88]

Although Adamson did what he could to inspire his troopers and to provide them with some soldierly skills, he also strove to maintain a high degree of discipline, a practice that he continued from his days in Halifax and probably before. If he at times appeared friendly and lax with his men, he never let this occasional informality become the norm. His efforts in this regard were apparently quite successful for in terms of crime, "I have had none," although this is probably an exaggeration. As before, he maintained order through vigilance and his willingness to punish transgressors. In disgust, he related to Mabel:

> On board the Idaho I reduced Sergeant Instructor Bertram to a Corporal for going on shore at Port Elizabeth. This morning he reported sick, and the hospital return has just come in and the brute has a filthy disease caught from a dirty woman at Capetown. He has to be left behind. He was married the day before he left Ottawa and I have been very good to him, although he was never of much assistance to me.[89]

Agar was so sickened with the sergeant's conduct that he opined, "I think men who subject themselves to such chances when they are on a game of this sort ought to be publicly disgraced as they are very short of traitors."[90]

Being willing to fall back upon his rank when required, Adamson also knew when to cede some of his authority to those beneath him. Before assuming their duties in the field, the draft was allowed to choose their own horses from a remount depot. Unlike the regiment proper, the draft did not bring horses with it from Canada, but rather arranged to be so equipped once in South Africa. After selecting a number of horses for himself, he "picked five of my men to pick the other 40." Since most of his troopers were originally from the West and thus probably knew more than he did about equine matters – as will be recalled, he had a number of "bronco hustlers" with him – he deferred to their better knowledge and ability in this instance. Although familiar with horses, he was after all an excellent rider, he probably did not feel comfortable selecting the horses upon which his men would depend when engaging the enemy.[91] To be fair, however, his devolution of authority *after* he had chosen his own mounts suggests that he may simply have desired to capitalize on the present situation by selecting the very best for himself and leaving his rejects for the men to squabble over. Rank certainly had its privileges during the war and the selection of horses may have afforded him the opportunity to exercise his prerogative to his ultimate advantage. And further still, his actions may have served yet another purpose. By allowing his men to choose their own mounts, he effectively shielded himself from any future recrimination if their horses proved to be inadequate; his men could complain to him about the quality of their four-legged transport, but they could not blame him for providing worthless mares as they had been responsible for selecting them initially. It is doubtful, however, that he would have allowed his men to ride horses that were obviously unsuited for the tasks at hand. All in all, this was a brilliant move on Adamson's part for he gave his men a significant responsibility from which they surely derived great satisfaction. The fact that the historical record is largely devoid of any significant complaints about these horses indicates that they performed this duty well.

The stress that Adamson seems to have been feeling at this point, when first becoming acquainted with the rigours and difficulties of wartime service, did not recede quickly. When he and his men were ordered to "Charleston alone to scout the country," he accepted the responsibility, but was somewhat uncertain as to his abilities to execute the same. He later wrote to Mabel, "They are asking a good deal of me. They offered me the job, asked me if I could do it, which of course I said I could, my only chance."[92] Such a statement insinuates that Agar felt that he and the draft had to somehow prove their competence and worth to their British brothers. Whatever his private opinions may have been, he appeared outwardly confident and able, an image that must have reassured his followers. By at least suggesting that he could handle such tasks, he encouraged his subordinates to trust in him; had he panicked or appeared incompetent, however, his men would surely have doubted his ability to lead them successfully and they may not have followed him with the same amount of zeal. Of course, declining to scout ahead would have marked Adamson as a less-than efficient officer and, given his ambitions, he was not about to assume this moniker without just cause. Demonstrating his ability, conversely, ensured that his career in South Africa would at least start on a solid foundation.

Shortly after his foray to Charleston, the draft was attached to a fighting column and began actual field operations. Their duties on the march consisted primarily of acting as either rear or advance guards, or as flanking parties or scouts, to the main body.[93] Their lack of training in open warfare soon became readily apparent as Adamson observed, "The men are all well and fit but some of them of very little use."[94] While teaching soldiers aboard ship may have sufficed for drill, physical fitness and marksmanship, it certainly did not do when it came to imparting the knowledge necessary to move quickly and effectively in the field on horseback. Being ahead of the main column, one of his duties was also to commandeer supplies and to search farmsteads for weapons or other items of value. As he once noted, "Went ahead, with authority to sack a certain Rebel[']s house, which we did most thoroughly."[95] After arriving in Standerton on 2 July 1900,[96] the draft was attached for duty to the South African Light Horse (SALH).

This association, albeit a temporary one, was indeed a fortunate blessing. Owing to the dearth of real and meaningful training that the men had received up to this point – it would seem that they were very much expected to learn on the job – Adamson was genuinely pleased to see that "My men are learning many tips from them."[97] Faced with the imminent prospect of meeting the enemy, Agar put his "two troops on fighting footing, cancelled all acting appointments and made new ones and fewer, doing away with Carey and three other Lance Corporals who had failed to have any authority over their small commands."[98] In this regard, Agar appears to have been concerned, and perhaps worried, about the draft's effectiveness. By replacing those whom he considered unable to lead, with presumably better-qualified or at least more promising soldiers, he demonstrated that competence would be *the* guiding principle since only the best and brightest would be advanced to positions of responsibility; he carried this attitude throughout his lengthy military career. Even though Agar had prepared the draft for action, he would still have to wait a little while longer to meet the enemy since "Lt. Adamson's party are forty miles in rear but cannot come on [to join the regiment proper] at present owing to the danger of capture by the Boers who are to be seen occasionally."[99] The small, scattered parties of Boers would indeed prove to be trouble as events would show.

Canada's Second Victoria Cross of the War – Wolve Spruit

When attempting to link with the main body of Strathconas, who always seemed to be one step ahead of the draft, Adamson's men met with their first real engagement of the war at Wolve Spruit, located some distance from Standerton. Since arriving in South Africa and assuming their duties as scouts and guards for various columns, they had not yet confronted the Boers in any sustained manner. This action would ultimately test the training that they had received since leaving Ottawa. For Agar, this confrontation with the enemy represented the very engagement that he had desired all along. Like his men, he too would find it a trying and difficult experience.

From Adamson's recollection of events, both immediately after the action itself and some months later, he and his draft, along with a large party from the SALH, started from Standerton early in the morning of 5 July and headed northeast toward a party of Boers on their right flank "who were showing in small numbers at top of hill." As the column approached, the "Enemy vanished with the supposed idea of drawing us into a trap." [See Map 2, Sketch 1].

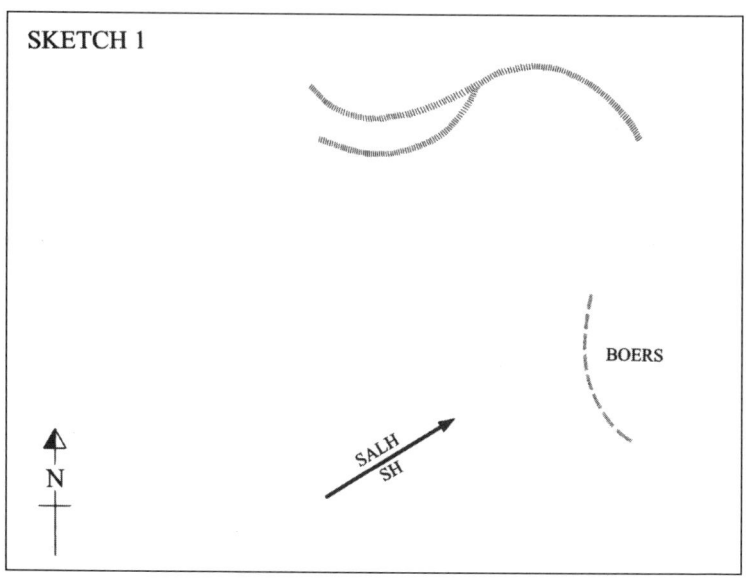

Map 2, Sketch 1: The Approaching Battle.

At this point, a small party of the SALH was detached from the main body and placed in hiding at the base of the hill on which the Boers had positioned themselves. The elevated heights provided them with a commanding view of the "open and undulating" terrain and allowed all movements below to be easily observed. Some of the remaining SALH, who carried with them a Maxim gun and a number of wagons, proceeded north-by-northwest, the idea being to lure the Boers off of the hill to pursue the Canadians, thus capturing them with the smaller force that had been concealed from view. A third detachment of the SALH was withdrawn a little and eventually circled back toward Standerton from whence they had just come, their purpose being unknown, although they may likewise have been attempting to lure the Boers from safety. Later on, this small body returned to the scene of the fighting and they, along with the other SALH left beneath the hill, engaged the Boers in this general area. A chess game of sorts was rapidly developing on the field, with each side attempting to outwit the other by strategically placing their forces in those areas where they might meet with the most success. Unfortunately, the northernmost body of the SALH moved too far to the north and thus lost contact with the Strathconas, thus negating any support that they might have offered. Seeing these movements, however, the Boers wisely remained on the hilltop, thus causing the ruse to fail. With more Boers appearing on his left flank, Adamson altered course to move against this new position in the north, thus leaving the concealed SALH to keep the enemy that had been sighted first in check. [See Map 2, Sketch 2].[100]

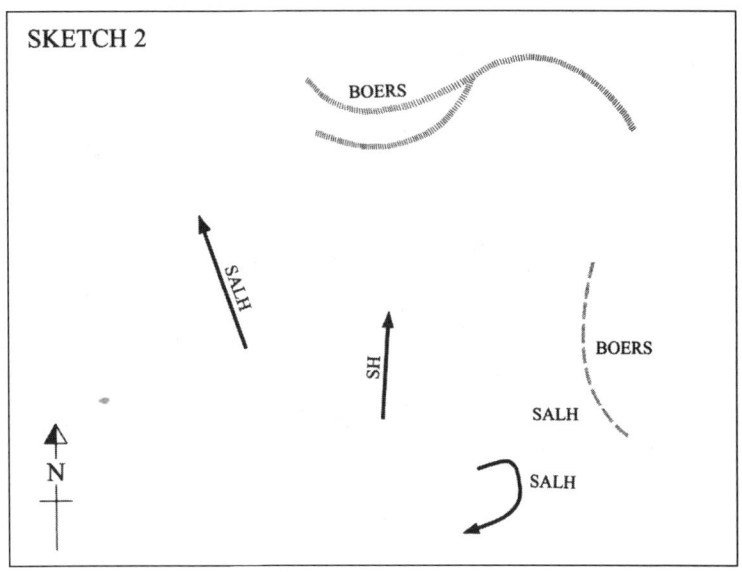

Map 2, Sketch 2: Splitting the Force.

To make his thrust, Agar deployed 17 of men in an advance guard at 50 yard intervals from one another, supported 500 yards back by the remainder of his draft. [See Map 2, Sketch 3]. Suddenly, from a range of about 3,000 yards, the Strathconas in the advance guard came under an intense fire from their front. The men in

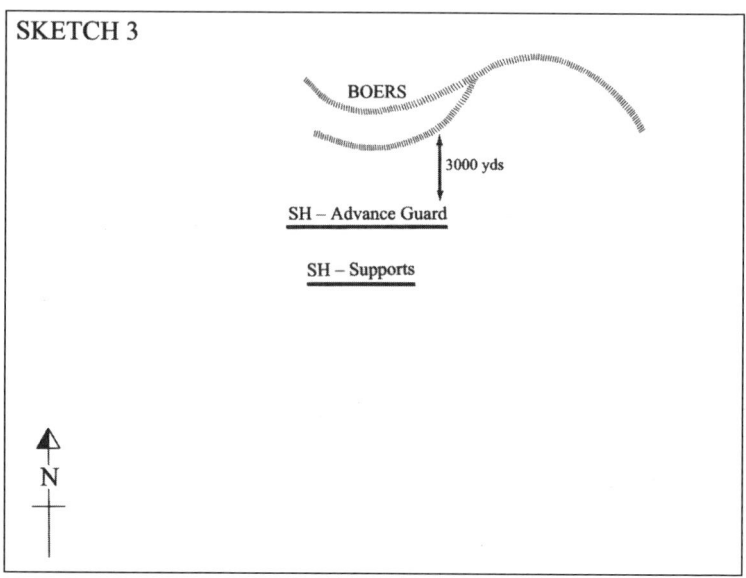

Map 2, Sketch 3: The Strathconas Prepare.

the rear rank (the supports in reserve) were brought up even with those who were leading. In an attempt to carry the hill, the entire body galloped forward to within 1,000 yards of the enemy. After advancing a fair distance, Adamson's horse was shot in the leg, thus forcing him to dismount and to move on foot to within 500 yards of the position from which the enemy was directing their shot. To further compound the Strathconas' difficulties, more Boers appeared to the north on their right flank; the enemy was now positioned in a horseshoe-like formation around the advancing Canadians. Despite the increased volume of fire, Adamson and his men continued to approach and engage the enemy to their front, moving to within 300 yards of the hilltop. [See Map 2, Sketch 4].

Because none of the SALH had supported the attack, they in fact were nowhere to be seen, Adamson could not overrun the Boer position and was eventually forced to retire. He had essentially

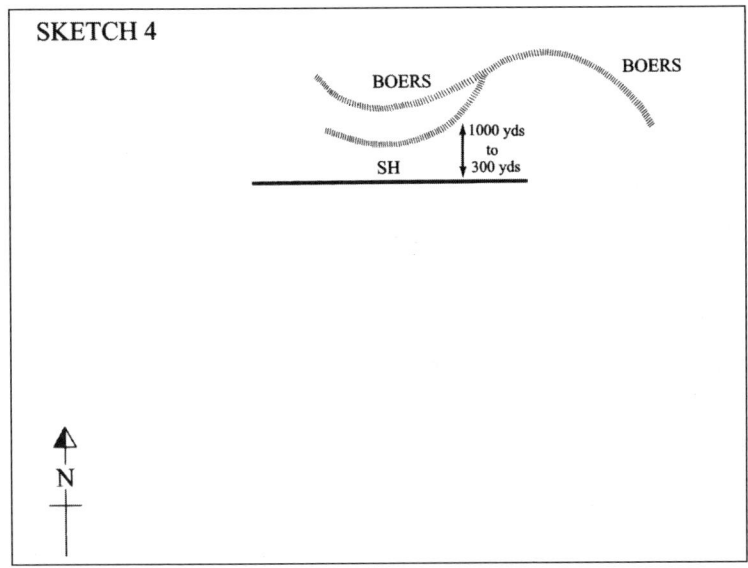

Map 2, Sketch 4: The Strathconas Advance.

advanced himself too far forward, thereby exposing both of his flanks: the SALH on his left had moved too far north and to the west to be of any value and those concealed on his right, who were positioned to capture the Boers coming off of the hill, had meanwhile engaged the enemy to their immediate front, with the assistance from the group that had originally left in the direction of Standerton, and were pushing them eastward, thus increasing the distance between themselves and Adamson. In light of the mounting casualties to both horses and men, Agar fell back to a position some distance away from the enemy to his front. Unfortunately, two of his troopers did not see this sudden movement and continued to advance; they were easily captured by the Boers and made prisoners.

During the general retreat, when most of the men had withdrawn to a safe distance [See Position 1, Map 2, Sketch 5] Sergeant A.H.L. Richardson noticed that Alex McArthur had been dis-

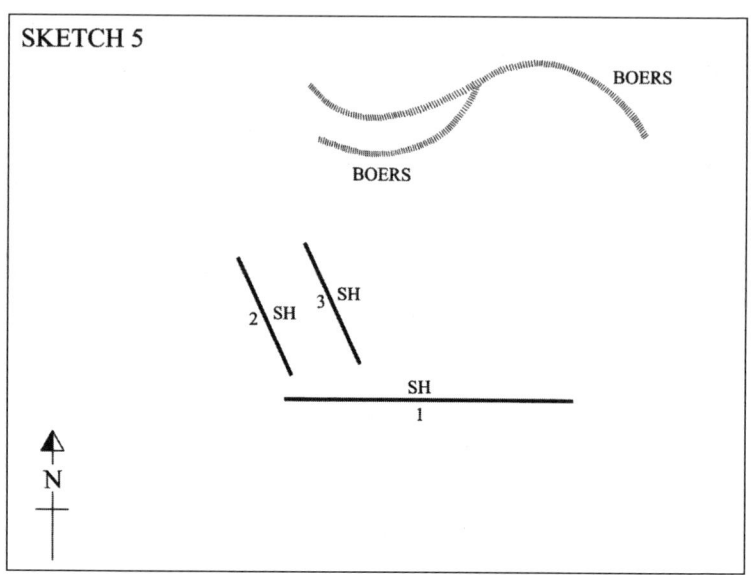

Map 2, Sketch 5: Concluding Movements.

mounted, wounded and left behind. To prevent him from being captured, the sergeant rode headlong into the advancing Boers who had by now left the safety of the hilltop and were giving chase, placed him on his horse and rode slowly back in the direction of the waiting Strathconas, all the while under continuous fire. Seeing Richardson and McArthur coming toward him, Adamson ordered George Sparkes, his good friend from Ottawa, and a few others who happened to be close by, to provide as much protection as their rifles would allow. As Agar later learned, Sparkes was wounded and could barely tilt his head to properly aim his rifle.

In order to avoid the cross fire that was coming from his front and right, Agar swung his remaining men around to a position on his left. [See Position 2, Map 2, Sketch 5]. Mounting some extra horses, he advanced somewhat in a north-easterly direction and gained a position which he held until nightfall, the "Enemy fearing to advance, thinking we had strong reserves." [See Position 3, Map 2, Sketch 5]. Once he had consolidated his position, he sent some men back to Standerton at a full gallop in order to bring up reinforcements and an ambulance to tend to the injured. All in all, Adamson thought that his men had behaved "wonderfully cool" throughout their first major engagement. As he later scrawled to Mabel, "The bullets simply flew all around your head and body. It is wonderful how any escaped." He reassured her, as he was apt to do, "I do not think I was afraid."[101]

Adamson's account of the engagement, on which this brief description is largely based, suggests a sense of orderliness and control. As revealed by the complexity of the draft's movements – breaking into two lines, advancing as one and then retiring, followed by shorter advances in spurts – his directions were apparently heard and understood by all, except the two who were captured. Again in his reassuring tone, he related to Mabel, "The men obeyed my whistle signals wonderfully well, and appeared to do good shooting." From his perspective, the draft's failure to capture the hilltop resulted from the fact that the SALH had not supported his advance. In essence, they had played a very minor role in the action; had they brought their superior numbers and Maxim to bear, the situation might have been concluded in a very different manner. Without the required support, Agar and his men were left to fend for themselves, certainly not an advantageous situation considering their lack of experience and the Boers' superior position. As if to justify his actions, he wrote, "I obeyed my orders, and the C.O. of the S.A.L.H. complimented me. My orders were to engage the enemy," he recalled, "and await reinforcements…none of whom arrived."[102]

Another description of the engagement, written by a Strathcona who participated in the fighting, offers an entirely different perspective and, it would seem, places much of the blame for the day's failure squarely on Adamson's shoulders. Thomas Easton Howell, who must have been on the extreme right of the line that Adamson established in front of the enemy against which they eventually advanced in force, as judged by his description of events, suggests that the action was actually quite chaotic and confusing. His account more or less parallels the general sequence of events that Adamson offers. He recalled that when the SH came under fire from the front for the first time, at a range of 3,000 yards or so, "Instead of proceeding cautiously the advance was continued at a gallop and ten minutes later we found ourselves scattered along a wide open ridge, without any support, and exposed to the fire of a rapidly increasing number of Boers." Soon thereafter, events continued to deteriorate for:

> ...our fellows had realized that they were in a tight corner but no one knew were Adamson was, no orders were given, and part of the troop was in a very exposed position on the wrong side of a barbed wire fence. A few minutes more and we would all have been completely surrounded. The only thing to do, of course, was to bolt and the whole troop was soon galloping away in all directions. At the next ridge some of us pulled up and waited for the stragglers two of whom were riding one horse.[103]

The two stragglers, of course, were Richardson and McArthur.

Certainly, Howell believed that Adamson had not conducted the operation in a competent and cool manner. The fact that he could not be seen by those who were looking for direction may have resulted from the unfortunate fact that "I was dressed as a trooper without a bandolier, but they [the Boers] were on to me all the time."[104] The loss of his horse, which compelled him to advance on foot, may also have played a role in reducing his visibility since his galloping troopers would have quickly outdistanced him. If, however, the Boers knew that Adamson was in a position of responsibility, he must have been directing his soldiers in a visible fashion that was clearly noticeable despite his attempts at an inconspicuous dress. Although Howell likewise recalled that "Something went wrong … and our support soon completely lost touch with us and did not turn up again," his passing reference to this point, and his concentration on the chaos of the action itself, implies that he blamed Adamson for much of what went wrong.[105] Agar may have acted somewhat impulsively and hastily, being in action for the first time, but as he stated, he was ordered to engage the enemy to his front and that was exactly what he did.

Interestingly, the Strathconas were not entirely unaccustomed to the type of duties that they were performing on the morning of 5 July. Only a few days earlier, and even before that, they had been scouting for the enemy in advance of a larger column. While spotting the occasional party of Boers, they neither gave chase nor engaged them in any concerted manner. On this point, Adamson observed before the action at Wolve Spruit, "The Boers although popping up all around did not show fight and I did not attack being in too small numbers and fearing being led into an ambush."[106] Judging by this comment, Agar at least possessed a rudimentary understanding of Boer tactics and very much desired to engage the enemy, but on his own terms and on ground that afforded him the advantage. His pursuit of the Boers on 5 July seems attributable, then, to the fact that he had been ordered to do so, in contrast to days before where the decision whether or not to engage the enemy apparently rested with him alone. The confidence instilled by larger numbers – the Strathconas and the SALH – might have provided further justification for his actions, for while he was outnumbered on this earlier occasion, he could at least rely (theoretically) on the support of the South Africans when pursuing the Boers north of Standerton.

In recalling the day, Trooper Frank Macmillan from McGill University likewise reinforced many of the facts surrounding the engagement:

> Last Saturday thirty-four of us were sent out as an advance guard to the South African Light Horse. When we got about twelve miles out and were four miles ahead of them, we saw seven Boers on a hill about a mile away. We started after them, and the beggars ran away and led us right into it, and I tell you we had all the fight we wanted for over an hour. The bullets fell like hail all around us and we lost two men, a sergeant and a trooper, whose horses were shot and who fell under the animals when we were retiring. There were also three men wounded and seven other horses shot. I had a bullet go through my coat and sweater, and it made a tear just like a cut with a knife.[107]

Similarly, writing some years later, Andrew Miller recorded the action in his history of the SH in South Africa. His account reinforces Howell's statements that all was not as orderly as Adamson contended. He wrote in 1912:

> On July 5th, at Wolverspruit [sic], near Standerton, thirty-eight troopers of Strathcona's Horse started in pursuit of an apparently small Boer force. The chase had not proceeded far, when the Canadians discovered themselves in an ambush, with over two hundred of the enemy on either side of them, who opened fire at less

than three hundred yards range. The Boer fire plainly indicated that the Canadians were outnumbered, and that their only safety lay in a speedy retreat.

He continued that once Richardson had grabbed McArthur, his horse, being tired and exhausted, would not leap over a single strand of barbed wire that stood about two feet off of the ground and which once formed part of a three-wire fence. Richardson spurred his horse but to no avail. Only when his mount received a wound in its shoulder did the shock of the impact impel it to jump the remaining wire and to make for the Canadian lines. After conveying the two soldiers to safety, the horse later died of its wounds and the exhaustion of the chase. While waiting for the horse to jump, "The Boers…were reducing the distance, and the Canadians could again hear their calls to surrender."[108]

After the engagement had been concluded, Adamson returned to camp and pondered these recent events. Being impressed by Richardson's bravery, he immediately forwarded a report to headquarters recommending that he receive the Victoria Cross (VC), the British Empire's highest award for bravery, believing "it would be a great thing if we could get him a V.C. for Canada, the S.H. and the Mounted Police to which he belongs."[109] In due course, Richardson received his decoration, the citation reading:

> On July 5, at Wolve Spruit, about 15 miles north of Standerton, a party of Lord Strathcona's Corps, only 38 in number, came into contact, and was engaged at close quarters, with a force of 80 of the enemy. When the order to retire had been given, Sgt. Richardson rode back under a very heavy cross-fire and picked up a trooper whose horse had been shot and who was wounded in two places, and rode with him out of fire. At the

time when this act of gallantry was performed, Sgt. Richardson was within 300 yards of the enemy, and was himself riding a wounded horse.[110]

This action was later described as "one of the most daring feats of the entire war."[111] Incidentally, Richardson was an original member of the Strathconas who had served previously with the NWMP. Owing to a back injury sustained whilst unloading horses from a transport ship, he had been left behind in hospital and later joined the draft in order to reconnect with the main body. He was one of the new men that Adamson had received at Maitland Camp before moving inland.

During this brief engagement, from the time that the enemy was initially observed until the concluding act of gallantry, two men were wounded and three were taken prisoner.[112] Despite the casualties, Adamson thought the day very beneficial, for the draft "are all working well, and the scrap has had a very good effect, making them look upon the game as not a joke ... but a very serious matter."[113] The encounter seemed to bring everyone, Adamson included, to the full reality of the nature of conflict. They had matured quickly in the span of a few hours and now better understood the complexities of war. Having no experience with the Boers in particular, or with fighting in general, the engagement undoubtedly came as a profound shock to all and gave them much to reflect upon. The remainder of Agar's time in South Africa could now be approached with the knowledge that command was not easy, especially in battle, and that orders, if poorly given, could have devastating consequences for those who were obliged to follow them.

With limited evidence on which to base an assessment, it is difficult to state with absolute certainty how much Adamson's conduct contributed to the defeat on 5 July. On the one hand, judging by the resulting effectiveness of the Boer ambush and the number of casualties that they inflicted, he appears to have acted hastily in ordering his men to the attack. Rushing forward, realizing that he was outnumbered and then retreating in haste is not suggestive of a well-conceived plan. While "dash and daring" were qualities certainly desired in officers, attributes that Agar later demonstrated he possessed in abundance, he might have realized on this occasion that his lack of battle experience warranted some initial caution. Yet, conversely, he seems to have been in the vanguard of the attack. Owing to the complexity of the draft's movements, his troopers must have heard his whistles; the Boers certainly knew that he was in charge. Agar was definitely not hanging back and directing the fight from the rear, but was rather leading from the front, again one of his most prominent attributes. From the above description, it seems logical to assume that Adamson's conduct on this occasion was the best that could be expected of an untested officer. He made some mistakes, but his men generally performed well under his direction. Now with their first engagement concluded, they could approach the remainder of their time in South Africa with the confidence borne of experience. No longer would they have to ponder how they would perform in battle or what battle itself would be like. A weight had finally been lifted.

Agar's Remaining Time in South Africa

After this defining engagement, Adamson continued his journey to join the regiment proper. When not actively engaging the enemy or writing home to tell Mabel about his novel experiences, he thought about the recent action and analyzed not only his own performance, but that of his men as well. Agar had reason to be proud of their collective accomplishments considering that it was their first real test of their soldierly abilities, but the incurred costs weighed heavily on his mind. In terms of casualties, this single engagement would ultimately prove to be one of the Strathconas' worst of the entire war, although no one was killed.[114] Adamson attempted to ensure in the days that followed that he and his soldiers would not be lured into an ambush for a second time. In this regard at least, he had learned a great deal about Boer tactics and, more importantly, about the difficulty of leading soldiers in battle and of leading well. Given these circumstances, he now approached his work with a little more caution than before, being acutely aware that his decisions could exact a heavy toll on those for whom he was responsible. Nearly a week later, on 10 July and again on 14 July, the draft recognized a number of Boers in the distance while scouting but did "no firing," nor did they give chase.[115]

The difficulties and hazards of campaigning, which the engagement at Wolve Spruit vividly illustrated, resulted in Agar becoming more forthright and assertive toward his superiors. Being now aware of how quickly situations could deteriorate in the field, he was much more reluctant to accept direction without first anticipating the possible outcomes. Rather than trying to impress his superiors with his willingness to engage the enemy, as had been the case when the draft was given the responsibility of scouting near Charleston shortly after their arrival in South Africa, he now conducted himself with the knowledge of a veteran, albeit a recent one, who could to some extent predict possible problems. His naïvety had been replaced by a soberness that had an eye to the future. On 10 July, for instance, he immediately objected to the nature of his orders after being instructed to escort a convoy of baggage. Although he dutifully "Reported that I was ready to go ahead," he was understandably concerned about the possible dangers owing to "my small knowledge of the direction we were to go in [and] that we were a bit small, as the men of the Devons [Devonshire Regiment] had gone on ahead by train."[116] When later ordered to scout ahead to locate the enemy, he again refused until he had obtained wire cutters, a tool that would enable his force to cut through fences to pursue (or flee from) the enemy.[117] The action at Wolve Spruit may have been playing on his mind at this moment since the wire fences in the area had proven a significant obstacle for some of his men. With only Agar's perspective on the issue, it is exceedingly difficult to gauge the reasons behind his increased hesitancy. Nevertheless, these two successive "objections" raise the possibility that he was somewhat shaken by his first engagement and therefore a little reluctant to meet the enemy again, especially when he was disadvantaged owing to the lack of proper equipment, available reinforcements and information about the terrain. On the other hand, however, his initial unwillingness to follow his orders could also be indicative of a well-developed moral courage in which he risked his own reputation (and possibly his career) for a point of principle that he felt deserved strong voice. He certainly had the best interests of his men in mind when informing his superiors of the potential dangers of their orders, for he admitted candidly, "I do not want to have my good men shot down for the sake of a few waggons of bulley beef and biscuits."[118]

Whatever his reasons for objecting, Adamson took decisive measures to ensure that his next engagement would not be accompanied by significant casualties or defeat. Wolve Spruit would not be repeated. In this regard, he continued with his desire to train his men to the best of his ability whenever time and resources permitted. On 12 July, he noted, "Took my men out at 8 a.m....for two hours and a half teaching them to keep proper intervals and dressing when extending which they do not do very well."[119] Such a comment suggests that the men's spacing during the earlier engagement may not have been proper and may have, in the end, contributed to some of the difficulties that they had encountered during their brush with the Boers. After this exercise, he conducted dismounted drill, a kit inspection and then marched them to water. Once the men had completed a general fatigue, he ordered a saddling harness parade, an inspection of arms, and then he dismissed them for dinner, but not before "reminding them that in future they had better be more careful about keeping their distance and dressing when patrolling."[120] His exhausting and varied regimen on this day certainly seems more consistent with punishment than with meaningful and thoughtful training! In his estimation, mistakes that were made in the past would certainly not be made again.

True to form, Adamson maintained a strict discipline within his command, a trait that by now had become one of his strongest attributes. After receiving word that the Provost-Marshal had a man in custody who was "very drunk and trying to shoot all comers," Agar "had him put in the guard tent and am sending him under arrest to Col. Steel [sic] later. He was just returning from Hospital at Durban, and I hear is a general bad character."[121]

Aside from these incidents, the draft experienced little additional excitement on their way to join the main body of SH, which they finally did at Watervaal on 17 July. Their arrival after such a long journey elicited little comment amongst the men who had served with the regiment from the outset. George Bowers, for instance, simply noted in his diary, "The draft have joined."[122] Years later, Steele recalled:

> Lieutenant Adamson, with 38 men and 40 horses, reported to me as a reinforcement from Canada. They had been sent by Lord Strathcona to fill up casualties,

and were a very good lot. I posted them to the regiment at once, keeping them in a troop under Adamson.[123]

Once the men of the draft had had sufficient time to prove themselves, Steele became a little more forthcoming in his praise. As he would later write, "I was very much pleased with their appearance and their conduct since has proved them to be a good class of men and interested in the work."[124] Although Steele's comments are few, they nevertheless provide insight into some of his own leadership abilities. Apparently understanding the fact that soldiers tend to work better under those with whom they are familiar and in whom they trust, he sent the draft to the field under their own officer, rather than dividing them amongst the regiment as a whole. However, each of the troops and squadrons under Steele's command had been recruited along territorial lines and so his actions in this regard may simply have been an attempt to keep those men from the same area of Canada together, as had been done throughout the rest of the regiment. By maintaining the draft's integrity, he nevertheless avoided the difficulties that Adamson's men would have faced when attempting to integrate themselves into a pre-existing team that was already functioning well. Such disruptions would not have proven beneficial to either.

That Steele thought the draft "a very good lot" and "a good class of men" suggests that Adamson had done a fine job in transforming his western recruits into an efficient body and that, for the most part, they trusted him. To be sure, the time that he had spent with them, both in conversation and in training while *en route* to South Africa, facilitated this end. That they had shared their first battle together probably reinforced their connection with their leader, and he with them, for everyone in the draft now shared a common experience around which they could solidify. Agar was apparently quite happy with the present arrangements for he wrote Mabel, "Have been given my draft as a separate command."[125] This situation, however, did not last, as the draft was taken from him less than a month later.[126] As he noted with some disappointment, "The draft was broken up on leaving Paarde Kop, as it gave one Squadron 5 troops. I am in command of No 4 Troop, A Squadron, with 12 of my old lot. I picked the best.... The others are drafted into different troops."[127] With the regiment being actively engaged in operations at this time, neither Steele nor Adamson had much opportunity to give the newly arrived draft any additional training. Rather, they were integrated into the larger whole and, like the others, were very much expected to learn "on the job."

Once Adamson joined the balance of the regiment, he more or less disappears from the historical record, save for his letters to his wife that unfortunately end in mid-August; he is not heard from again until some months later. The near total lack of references to his later performance suggests, at first glance, that he was neither so outstanding as to deserve public compliment, nor so incompetent as to warrant public censure. Rather than operating as a separate entity, his fate and fortunes were now tied to that of the Strathconas themselves, and this fact, combined with his valuable experiences to date, may have removed some of the pressures that he had been feeling. In contrast to his time at Maitland, he now had other officers to assist him in his work. For at least the next month, he continued with the various duties that he and his men had performed since arriving in South Africa. Writing to Mabel, he noted, "Our particular work is to either scout, protect [the] column or gallop up, drawing the fire of the enemy, [and] pretending to retire, endeavouring to draw them out in the open."[128] Other duties also included "rebel chasing, farm burning, and collecting civilians for shipment to concentration camps."[129] Despite these general responsibilities, he was nevertheless involved in the capture of three different towns in quick succession.

In August, in one of his first major actions after Wolve Spruit, Adamson and his soldiers played a key role in capturing Amersfoort. Outlining the general situation for his wife, Agar wrote, "I had the advance guard and 2 small galloping guns under me, with orders to enter if possible, if not hold for main column (flying) to come up." With understandable pride, he also recalled for her benefit, "I was the first to reach the actual Town being in the centre of the semi circle the advance guard formed."[130] His comments quite clearly indicate that he led from the front on this particular occasion, and by so doing, set the example for all others to follow. Being conspicuously exposed, he encouraged his troopers to follow him as he implied through his actions and presence that he was willing to share the same amount of risk as they. The relative ease with which Amersfoort was captured prompted Steele to write after the war, "The behaviour of the regiment on this occasion was excellent. The whole of it screened the front and flanks during the march, and by skilful work on the part of the corps the enemy's positions were turned and he was forced to retire." Perhaps more importantly, he also saw fit to mention that "The officers of the regiment worked so well that it would be hard to make individual mention."[131] Steele did not confine his praise entirely to his officers alone, for he noted that his soldiers "behaved splendidly displaying great caution."[132]

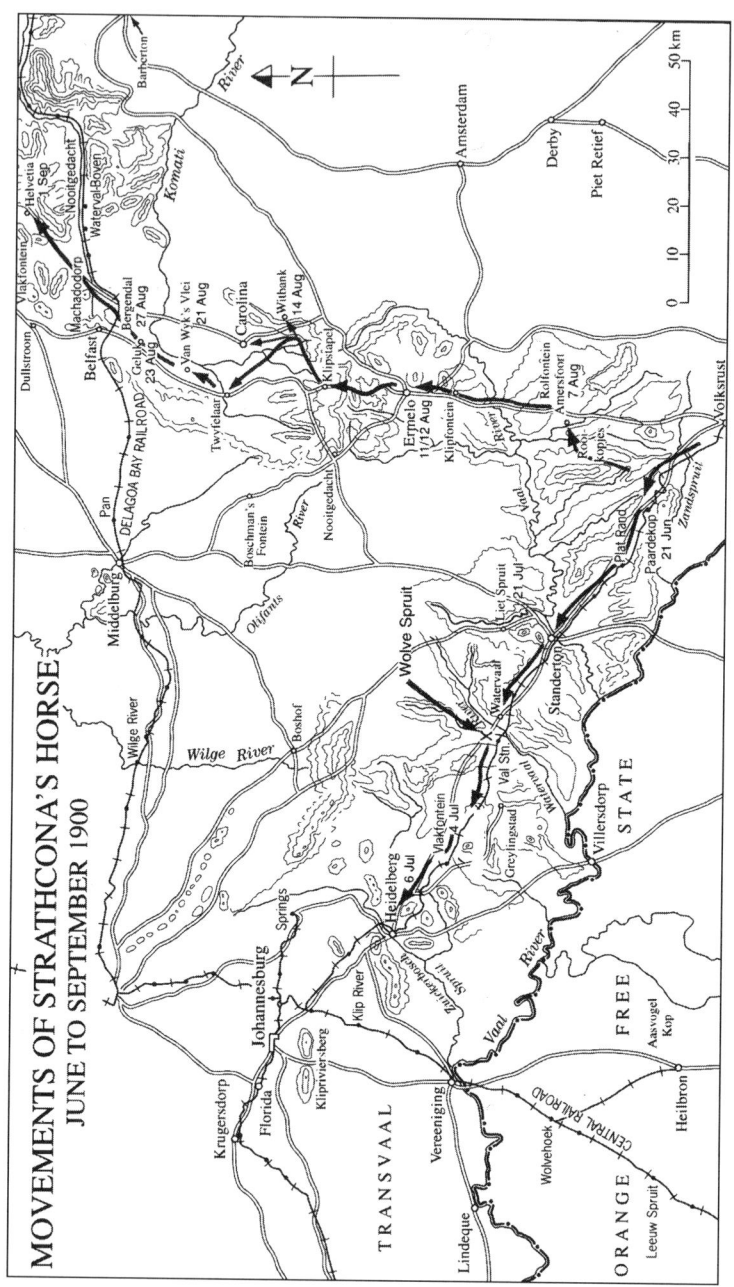

Map 3: Movements of Strathcona's Horse, mid-1900.

Adamson again led from the front as the SH approached the town of Emerlo. He later recalled, "I had a troop on the flank the next day, and owing to the advance guard mixing up their orders, got into Ermilo [sic] ahead of them." Not to be deprived of the benefits that by rights accompanied being first into town, Agar immediately commandeered one of the nicest houses and, much to his surprise and satisfaction, "It turned out to be owned by a very rich Hungarian Merchant who I found to be a Mason." While he and the other officers of the SH enjoyed this gentleman's company, aided in no small measure by "most excellent Claret ... and sweet champagne, a most comfortable bed, cigars and cigarettes," Adamson ensured that the occupying troops did not destroy the merchant's property by posting his men at key locations on his estate and throughout the town. While using his soldiers in this manner may seem unfair – Adamson clearly benefited the most – the men probably did not mind too much as some were allowed to sleep in the stables, rather than under the stars and clouds as they had been accustomed. Because of this exchange, "the brother lost nothing by being a Mason and we gained much."[133] Once these two towns had been captured, the SH moved against and captured Carolina where they "blew up the powder magazine."[134]

Adamson always seemed to be in the vanguard of the advance. When recalling the capture of Machadodorp, T.E. Howell, whom Agar had selected to remain with him when the draft was disbanded, noted, "My troop was first into the town and most of the men, hot and breathless with running, headed straight for the hotel where we helped ourselves freely to liquid refreshment and cigars." Later on in the day, after noticing a group of British soldiers "helping themselves to everything they could lay their hands on," the some men from SH "joined them in this congenial work and came out of the store with our pockets stuffed full of things."¹³⁵ Although Agar was not necessarily with his men while they plundered the town, he apparently turned a blind eye to their illegal activities. Had he attempted to intervene, he would have surely received their ire and spite for looting had by this time become a common practice in the regiment.

On 1 September, after the SH had begun their advance through a feature known as Crocodile Valley, they noticed a Boer convoy approaching a long and difficult slope at the other end of the ravine, an obstacle that would slow their progress and offer the pursuing British column a chance to capture many valuable stores and to seize many prisoners. After observing such a temping prize, some scouts belonging to SH "pushed their horses forward at the gallop until within four hundred yards of it." Lacking support and being mounted on now-tired horses, they were compelled to retire. Nevertheless, half an hour later:

> …a troop of Strathcona's Horse under Lieut. Adamson took up the pursuit, but the convoy had then reached the head of the valley and was disappearing among the hills. As the pursuit proceeded, the regiment followed at a rapid pace close behind. Overtaking the rear guard near a farm house at the foot of the hills, Lieut. Adamson and his men carried on dismounted action, but as the regiment was halted and ordered to go into bivouac he returned, although the scouts remained out until dark. The troop had retired some distance before it was discovered that one of its number, Pte. McGillivray, was missing. An attempt was made to find him, but the search was fruitless. The Boers had been quick to occupy the ground Lieut. Adamson had vacated, and had made the missing man a prisoner.¹³⁶

Six months later, Adamson learned for himself the true fate of his trooper whom he thought dead up until this point. His letter to Mabel, in which he relates much of the same story as above, offers an extraordinary glimpse into his character and leadership abilities and thus is worth quoting at length:

> My man McGillvery [sic] lost and supposed to be killed at Badfontein Valley has turned up in South Africa a returned prisoner. There has hardly been a day that I did not think I should have gone further into the enemy's lines to find him, although at the time had I done so and this I thoroughly understood we must have lost half our men and a whole squadron of the S.A.L.H. under a seasoned officer refused to even support us and declined to even remain with me which we did do for three hours after they left us. As things turned out my judgment was fortunately a proper one as they had a trap for us and not one of us could have pulled out alive had we fought for it, as I fancy we should. It now appears that McGillvray [sic] after passing the third donga (after which I thought all my men safe) and well out of fire, went off after some chickens he heard cackling and was collared by the enemy, who thought we would returned for him. Had I done so we would all have fallen into a trap and for the sake of a man who says the Boers treated him very well, and he was much more comfortable with them than with us, and was sorry when they were forced to give him up. It is just as well we did not. You have no idea darling how happy this piece of news has made me, and taken a great weight off my mind, for while it was by no means cowardice (much as you may doubt it, knowing how you fancy I value my skin) that prevented my rushing what I felt sure to be a trap. I had 50 men under me and only

myself to decide and did not wish to lead them into trouble. The next day I picked 12 men to go over the ground. The rest of this story you know. Anyway it has helped to make my reminiscences of S.A. [South Africa] less unpleasant than they were.[137]

Agar's private confessions to his wife, in which he could scarcely contain his joy, confirm that he was generally interested in and deeply concerned about the welfare of his soldiers. His admission that he felt responsible for the trooper's demise, as well as for the well-being of everyone else under his command, is very much in keeping with his character and personality. His comments further reveal that he valued life and did not wish to expose his soldiers to unnecessary danger, however noble and honourable the cause. He again implies that the pressure and solitude of command weighed heavily on his shoulders, but that some of this burden was alleviated by the news that all was indeed well. The relief he felt probably resulted in no small measure from his rationalization that any mistakes that he might have made, or any actions that he did not take, were now inconsequential and of little moment since the trooper was found safe, alive and very well cared for. If Adamson is to be criticized, it might be for failing to account for all of his men, but this expectation is probably somewhat unrealistic given the confusion that would have occurred during the action in question and the fact that McGillivray went off on his own accord without informing others of his intentions.[138] Agar's concern for his men was not simply a literary ploy to gain credit with and sympathy from his wife, as T.E. Howell in recalling the action later wrote, "Finally Adamson unwilling to imperil the safety of all for the sake of one gave the order to retire and the troop rode reluctantly away. Once out of range, however, we halted and examined the surrounding country for signs of the missing man."[139]

Unfortunately, very little is known about Adamson's activities during the months of September and October.[140] Because his correspondence from this period has not survived, there is very little to say about his specific involvement in the Strathconas' subsequent engagements. The fact that his subordinates neither recorded his activities nor their impressions of him in their personal reflections only complicates the matter further.[141] Agar's conduct, along with that of the remainder of the regiment, was sufficient enough to encourage Lord Strathcona to write after the war:

> It is hardly necessary for me to say that I am very proud of Strathcona's Horse. The men were evidently all that could be desired and I have every reason to be grateful for the way in which they were led by the Officers who were appointed to command them.[142]

All in all, given his past record, he probably continued to lead from the front while at the same time keeping the welfare of his soldiers foremost in mind. If his past behaviour is any indication, he surely maintained discipline within his troop and punished those who transgressed the bounds of acceptable conduct. Agar would have agreed with Steele's comment that "There are a few men who ought not to be in the corps, but strict discipline keeps them in order. No one can avoid getting men who have made a mistake in joining, such men thought war was a picnic."[143] According to one member of the draft, "The rovers and adventurers of no fixed occupation who always turn up when there are heads to be broken" were apparently "well represented" in the regiment.[144] Additional experience would have given Agar a better understanding of the difficulties of leading men against a determined enemy. That he had much to learn still is suggested by his admission to Mabel, "There are many tricks about campaigning, which had I know [sic], I would have bought several things."[145] Almost certainly, he continued to develop into a competent and trusted officer on whom his subordinates could depend. With additional time, Agar gained a further appreciation of the men whom he commanded. Although a man apart, being from a different class, he understood how to relate to his soldiers in a way to which they responded positively. Rather than rely exclusively on his rank and authority like some, he knew how to motivate them, such as by playing to their sense of pride and giving them significant responsibilities. Over the course of the next few months, he undoubtedly continued on this track and furthered his understanding of his men's needs, wants and desires.

While in South Africa, Adamson very much preferred the company of his British counterparts, with whom he seems to have become a favourite, than that of his own brother officers.[146] Perhaps owing to his upbringing, the time that he had spent at Cambridge and his subsequent relationships with many peers of the realm, he related better with the former than with the latter. Truly, he "had no difficulty whatever with the British officers, whom he preferred to his 'crude' and 'uncivilized' compatriots."[147] In his letters home, Agar gossiped frequently about many of his military (but in his opinion, not his social) superiors. Of the regiment's officers generally, he thought them "a very mixed lot."[148] In his estimation, because of this mediocrity, "The men are heartily sick of most of their officers who with few exceptions are…a most incompetent lot, very selfish, and most ignorant, and not particularly anxious to learn."[149] He likewise thought the surgeon "a shocking bounder."[150] Adamson, however, reserved his most caustic and venomous criticism for Steele, who, "lacking polish [is] generally rude to everybody."[151] Owing to his lack of respect for his CO, "I personally have not spoken a word to him except officially."¹⁵² At least from his perspective, he "made no enemies" amongst his brother officers despite his intense dislike of them.¹⁵³ His lack of rivals resulted from his unwillingness to publicly voice his dislike of those with whom he was forced to serve and his ability to maintain a façade that bespoke professionalism and cordiality. His private opinions, which contain an element of arrogance, remained guarded and were apparently never allowed to adversely affect his relations with his fellow officers. As he once related to Mabel, "I did my duty while playing the game under most trying circumstances often and always in most [uncongenial] company, but did not express my views."¹⁵⁴ What they thought of this well-bred and well-read Anglophile is unknown. While he remained loyal to his superiors in that he followed their orders and did not cause a noticeable amount of trouble, his approach could be described as dishonest and two-faced. From his candid admissions, it seems that Agar was a competent actor, being able to maintain an air of friendliness with his fellow officers, while internalizing an extreme aversion to their characters and personalities.

Invalided and Recuperation

In many of the "glorious little wars" that Great Britain fought during the nineteenth century, disease posed a much greater threat to life than did the enemy; the conflict in South Africa was indeed no different. On the veldt, enteric fever proved to be a significant problem as scores of soldiers either died from this malady or were sent to hospital to recover.¹⁵⁵ Within SH, the incidence of disease increased in September, October and November. George Bowers recorded in his diary that the regimental surgeon sent many to hospital in late-October owing to dysentery and other illnesses.¹⁵⁶ Steele similarly noted, "We have a great many suffering from slight attacks of fever, and dysentery, but none serious."[157] Being a constant threat to the regiment's strength and effectiveness, it was only a matter of time before illness of one sort or another claimed more victims. Having thus far escaped the enemy's guns, Adamson soon fell ill in early-November and was eventually sent to hospital to recuperate, a transfer that effectively ended his association with SH in the field. At the end of the month, after spending some time in hospital, he was invalided back to England.[158] Leaving Cape Town aboard the steamship *Oratava*,[159] he undoubtedly thought about being reunited with his wife, with whom he had corresponded so frequently, and also about the regiment in which he had served for roughly four months through an arduous and often frustrating campaign.

Once reunited with Mabel in London, the couple spent some time in the city together and then left in mid-January 1901 for "the south of Europe" where Agar hoped "to recover his health in the milder climate."[160] The time spent in France seems to have been the soothing salve that Agar required for word later reached Canada that he was "rapidly recovering his health and strength."[161] Being pleased with his progress, he also confessed, "Am bucking up down in this beautiful part of the country every day."[162] His convalescence allowed him and his new bride to continue their married life under more suitable and stable conditions, that is, together. Although married in November 1899, much of the following year had been occupied with Agar's pursuit of his military ambitions, whether in Halifax or South Africa. Unfortunately for them both, the time that they spent together in France did not last.

London

After recuperating sufficiently, Agar returned to London to attend to personal matters. When not attempting to pass his medical boards[163] or wrestle his pay from the WO, Adamson, true to form, spent much of his time cultivating his many refined interests and circulating in the refined atmosphere of high society. Meals at the Trocadero[164] and shopping excursions to Harrods[165] were mixed with attempted visits to Lady Dudly, Lord Strathcona and Lord Dundonald, in addition to Mrs. Hutton, the wife of Major-General Hutton, his old militia acquaintance.[166] Agar's military interests did not suffer either during his sojourn for he received dinner invitations from distinguished soldiers[167] and met briefly with "General Cleary under who I served for three weeks." Of this latter meeting, Agar boastfully recalled, "He was very nice and of the opinion that the Strathcona's [sic] should be turned into a School of Instruction to the English mounted troops."[168] Perhaps to his pleasure, he also spent some time gossiping about Steele's inappropriate and unbecoming behaviour at two luncheons given to the regiment by Lord Strathcona.[169]

Back in Canada

Adamson's stay in London ended with his return to Canada aboard the SS *Minnehaha* in March 1901. The company with whom he was forced to travel did not necessarily live up to the standard to which he had become accustomed. As he observed, "We have about 60 passengers, none of them look nice, and I greatly fear not much amusement to be got out of them."[170] His temporary confinement was soon ended, no doubt with much relief, upon his return to the familiar sights and personalities of upper-class Ottawa. Old activities that once provided him with much amusement were taken up again with renewed vigour and interest. Over the course of the next few months, Agar dined with the Speaker of the Senate and the head of the Geological Survey.[171] He also took in a "Very jolly little dinner at Government House," after which he "Had a talk to Their [Excellencies] after the rest had left."[172] Again, he did not let his military interests wane for he attended "a supper party at the Club...with some gentleman troopers of S.H."[173] Charity balls, riding parties, skating parties, a hunting trip to Quebec and his regular militia duties all served to occupy Agar during the months that followed his premature return from South Africa.[174] Many of his acquaintances in the city were quite happy to hear of his safe return for "The Masonic Lodge are presenting me with a really handsome pair of hair brushes."[175]

South Africa ... again

At least for the moment, Agar's ambition and quest for adventure would not let him settle back into the stately and privileged lifestyle that he had enjoyed prior to his first appointment. Perhaps a dinner given by the Governor General to commemorate the battle of Paardeberg rekindled or reinforced his desire for a commission that would again take him overseas to South Africa.[176] His military acquaintances in London may also have set his mind thinking about his return to the sun and sand, for while in the city, he begged Mabel, "if they ever again really want my advice and assistance, you will spare me won't you darling and pretend you like it."[177] Unlike before, however, when he could only rely on the goodwill and patronage of an impressive retinue of supporters and on the few practical skills that he had gleaned from the militia, he could now cite meaningful military experience as an additional qualification. The time spent with Strathcona's Horse, both with the draft and regiment proper, gave him a good appreciation of the confusion of war and, perhaps more significantly, of the difficulties of leading soldiers. The knowledge that he could now impart was based on real and relevant experience drawn from the present war, rather than from anecdotes or stories taken from policing or Canada's earlier military commitments such as the North-West Rebellion of 1885. The limited experience that he gained through the militia could only go so far in developing his ability as a competent and effective officer, yet his active service in South Africa, where casualties were incurred and the real demands of active campaigning were fully realized, provided him with a more complete, if quick, education. His experience, and consequent rise in credibility, was a point that he would not allow to go unnoticed by those whom he now petitioned.

In late-March 1902, with an air of confidence and certainty, Adamson wrote to the Minister of Militia and Defence, "I should like to place my services at your disposal again, and if you see fit to give me the command of a squadron, with the rank of Captain, in the contingent now being formed for South Africa, I shall be very proud to accept it." His brief appeal made note of the fact that the draft under his command had engaged the enemy on two separate occasions prior to joining the remainder of the regiment, with the obvious implication being that these engagements had both been successful. Adamson was also quick to note that he had recommended Richardson for the VC. Associating himself with a recent war hero provided some advantages as well, although he was wise to omit that his own lack of expertise had contributed to the situation in which Richardson had earned his decoration. Having briefly summarized the highlights of his short but eventful career in South Africa, he hoped that "I am not presuming in asking you to consider my claim for a captaincy."[178]

Approximately one week later, in early-April, Adamson composed a second petition that not only echoed many of the sentiments expressed in the first, but which also described his experiences in the Canadian militia, in Halifax and in South Africa, in much greater detail. Lieutenant-Colonel A.L. Jarvis, the CO of the GGFG and the individual to whom Adamson appealed for assistance, was so impressed by the accomplishments of the young veteran that he "strongly recommended" him for further consideration. "In further support of my claims for the appointment as a Senior Captain in the force about to be enrolled for active service," Adamson wrote, "I would state that I was appointed Lieutenant in Strathcona's Horse and was placed in sole command of a draft of 50 men sent from Canada to reinforce that Regiment. Of these the great majority had actually no military experience whatever." He also made it known that he had been "highly complimented by Colonel Byng in Regimental Orders" when attached to the SALH.[179] Such statements as these alluded to his leadership abilities for the reader was led to draw the natural conclusion that if the draft had been successful, then their accomplishments must have resulted in no small measure from the control and influence that Adamson exercised. As if his past experiences were not quite enough, he noted for effect, but perhaps somewhat needlessly, "I have an equitation certificate." In conclusion, he ventured "to hope that my special experience and service while in sole charge and command of this draft, and my subsequent service throughout the war and my record in the Active Militia of Canada may entitle me to be favourably considered in this request."[180]

To add to these petitions, Adamson also received recommendations from Lieutenant-Colonel W.E. Hodgins and Lieutenant-Colonel F. Toller, both of whom once commanded the GGFG. Ironically, his former CO in South Africa, Sam Steele, also offered his good praises for the young officer.[181] While Agar possessed little respect for the man,[182] he thought the drunkard-cum-bully a suitable and adequate choice to offer him a recommendation to further his ambitions. Approaching his former CO took considerable gall and clearly reveals that Adamson was not averse to advancing himself by those means that he deemed most likely to succeed, whatever they may have been. A glowing recommendation from a senior officer with field experience was truly a valuable piece of paper. The fact that Steele recommended Adamson at all is extremely interesting, especially given the latter's feelings and previous comments toward the former. Evidently, Adamson *did* keep his opinions to himself, so much so that Steele was entirely unaware of his subordinate's feelings toward him. A competent actor indeed! That a recommendation was offered suggests that the public and private relationship between the two men was fairly calm and cordial, despite an underlying animosity on Agar's part. If Steele had desired to see Adamson's career stymied, he could have offered a severe critique of the young officer or simply withheld comment altogether.

In due course, Adamson received a commission as a junior, not a senior, captain in the 6th Canadian Mounted Rifles (CMR).[183] When reading Agar's petitions, one can sense that he believed himself somehow "entitled" to a commission at a higher rank than before for, as he himself put it, he was making a "claim" for a captaincy. Unlike other petitioners, many of whom simply asked to be commissioned in whatever capacity possible so that they might serve in South Africa, Adamson was very particular as to *what* he expected from the government and *why* he should receive it. His experience led him to believe that he deserved favourable consideration and a rank that was more befitting of his station and qualifications. The time that he had spent on the veldt, if nothing more, certainly gave him additional confidence and an air of haughtiness.

As it turned out, Adamson was indeed a valuable asset to 6 CMR for it "contained a core of professional officers, [but] few had combat experience."[184] Although the CO and the Second-in-Command, Lieutenant-Colonel J.D. Irving and Major W.D. Gordon, respectively, were both professional soldiers, neither had served in South Africa. As before, "The officers chosen to command...were a mix of the tired, the trusted, and the ambitious. For many, an advancement in rank provided an inducement to join; all stood a good chance of exchanging their war experience for a promotion upon their return." To be sure, most of the men who were recruited to fill the ranks lacked any previous military experience, while the remainder "claimed only temporary and frequently nominal membership in the Canadian militia."[185] The opportunity thus presented itself whereby Adamson could impart advice to both those above and below him concerning the enemy, their style of warfare and what one could expect while on active service since he had "learned the wiliness of the Boers and knew when and how to strike."[186] In contrast to before, he could now impart more meaningful and realistic advice based on his own personal successes and shortcomings. His credibility as a veteran could now be put to good use in heightening the quality and usefulness of his sermons. Having experience with veteran soldiers also set him apart from others.

On 17 May 1902, 6 CMR left Halifax aboard the *Winifredian*, having spent minimal time in the city. Like the other contingents raised for service in South Africa, some of the time in transit was spent on drill, rifle practice and attending lectures on tactics. To the disappointment of some (and perhaps to the jubilation of others), peace was finally declared two weeks later, thus ending the war and the regiment's *raison d'etre*. Adamson reacted poorly to the news. Writing to Mabel, he made known from Durban that "I am severely disappointed not to have had a chance at doing something, and in this Regiment there would have been more of it than with the Strathconas."[187] A few weeks later, he similarly lamented, "You probably know the bad luck. We have all been ordered home at once."[188] His frustration must have weighed heavily, for his efforts in gaining a second commission had amounted to naught.

Although Agar did not have the opportunity to lead his subordinates against the enemy, the results of which might have confirmed if his earlier experiences had indeed made him a better officer, he certainly seems to have learned something from his first visit to South Africa. He observed in one of his letters, "We have done very little drilling, which is possible [sic] a mistake."[189] Apparently referring to 6 CMR as a whole, rather than to himself particularly, Agar acknowledged the value of undertaking some sort of training regimen when time and opportunity so permitted, although he understood that aboard ship, the resources and space required for meaningful instruction were at a severe premium. Despite these shortcomings, Adamson was "very well pleased with my Squadron."[190]

Seeing no possibility of active service, 6 CMR sailed home. Rather than return with his regiment, Agar decided to remain in South Africa to investigate farming opportunities and the possibility of obtaining a British commission. His agricultural schemes failed to come to fruition and, with some frustration and discontent reported, "I have tried in vain to get a Military job of any kind but they are firm and in spite of my being on the Reserve of Officers of the British Army, they will not employ over-seas Colonials."[191] After realizing that his future did not lie in this part of the world, he returned to Canada and his much beloved wife, thus ending his military service in the South African War.

Concluding Thoughts

After his two trips to South Africa, Adamson could fairly claim that he was an experienced and seasoned soldier. While his campaign medal would provide a "badge of social respectability" and a certain amount of credibility amongst his military acquaintances, both superior and subordinate alike, the lessons that he had learned about leadership, about soldiers in general and about himself in particular, were of much greater value. His service during the South African War certainly gave him much to reflect upon. Despite his early difficulties, he had reason to be proud of his accomplishments. All in all, he had led a draft of western-men with no military experience to South Africa without major incident, had led them through some difficult engagements with relatively few casualties, had provided the best training that space, time and resources would allow, had kept them in good, if not strict, discipline (although he sometimes may have turned a blind eye to looting!), and had become an efficient officer during his months with Strathcona's Horse and the 6th Canadian Mounted Rifles. Above all else, he apparently learned, or at least confirmed, a great deal about the nature of soldiers. Like other veterans, he understood that leading in active operations against an enemy was a demanding, if not a stressful, responsibility that required the greatest of care and concern. The pressure of actual battle demanded that he act more decisively, more forcefully, and more quickly than he ever had to in the past. Not surprisingly, he made a few initial mistakes, but made a determined effort to correct such deficiencies. During his time in South Africa, Agar acquainted himself with the nuances of leadership in the field and strove to become a better officer by learning from his own experiences, as well as from those of others.

Given his military interests and ambitions, it is perhaps fitting and appropriate that he was also connected with Canada's second Victoria Cross of the South African War. In many respects, he exemplified the type of man that many in turn-of-the-century society were encouraged to be: dashing, dapper, courageous and imperialistic. Indeed, one of *his* sergeants earned the empire's highest award for bravery under *his* command. In the years that followed, the story of how Arthur Richardson came to rescue a wounded mate was undoubtedly told and retold to inquisitive listeners at innumerable dinner parties and nightly soirees. Agar was a good storyteller and this was a good story. What he probably failed to mention though, was that his mistakes, to one extent or another, had led to the situation that forced Richardson to act in the first place. Had he not been so hasty in ordering his men forward, it is conceivable that this brave and gallant act would never have been required at all.

In the autumn of 1914, Agar returned to military service as a captain with the PPCLI. Over the next four years, he would rise to command his regiment, earn the Distinguished Service Order and ruin his health. While the pressure of command certainly weighed on him during his time in South Africa, when he met the Boers only occasionally and was responsible for a relatively small number of men, it eventually became unbearable during the First World War when he was accountable for an entire battalion that made constant and costly contact with the Germans. To be fair, however, neither war was comparable to the other. Until that time, however, Agar would have to content himself with what opportunities the Canadian militia afforded.

While his career with the PPCLI is certainly beyond the scope of this book, it seems reasonable to suggest, tentatively of course, that the leadership lessons that he learned in South Africa provided a strong foundation upon which much of his subsequent military behaviour was based. Having already learned many of the differences between leading citizen-soldiers in a militia setting and leading citizen-soldiers in the field against a determined enemy, he could now strive to replicate his successes while at the same time avoiding the paths that had earlier led to failure. In France and Belgium, Agar relied on many of the same leadership techniques that he had refined or developed in South Africa, probably because he found them to work so well. During both conflicts, for instance, he always spent time learning about those under his command since, in his opinion, "it is inclined to help the men if they know you take more than a general interest in them."[192] In addition, when serving in the trenches, he, as before, tried to limit the needless risk to which his soldiers were exposed.[193] During the First World War, Agar could usually be found in forward positions with his soldiers, a characteristic that he continued from his time in the vanguard of attacks in South Africa. As is sure, simply locating examples of duplicate behaviour between the two wars, of which there are more, does not conclusively prove that Agar used his earlier experiences to influence his subsequent conduct, but it is an intriguing possibility that certainly deserves attention.

In addition, some of his attitudes also changed as a result of his twenty years of service. Reflecting the common thought at the turn-of-the-century, for instance, he initially believed that officers should be men of station who possessed the right upbringing, background and schooling. Patronage was a means for advancement that should be exploited. In contrast, he realized during the Great War that some men from the ranks, regardless of their pre-war social standing or occupation, made very good officers or NCOs owing to the practical knowledge that they had accrued at the front. By this time, in his estimation, ill-used and ill-advised patronage had become a scourge to Canada's professional army and he often attempted to limit its pervasive and destructive influence.[194] This change in perception probably resulted from the many opportunities that he had had to watch his soldiers perform in the face of the enemy and that he himself had risen largely, if not exclusively, on merit. Seeing the successful manner in which they handled men in difficult and trying circumstances probably destroyed his preconceived notions that only the well-bred should be commissioned or advanced. The frequent need to replace casualties, something that he had not been forced to do in South Africa to any great extent, seems to have contributed to this realization as well by compelling him to select those individuals who were best suited to command, regardless of their social pedigree. During the First World War, when he was responsible for the success of the PPCLI, he certainly became more willing to sacrifice social graces and table manners for battlefield efficiency, although competency always remained a guiding principle.[195] Again, examining this and other attitudinal shifts in order to further understand his character would surely be profitable.

All in all, Agar was a dynamic individual who developed significantly as a leader over time. He was neither static nor inert in his thinking, for he learned from past lessons and allowed them to guide his future conduct, at least in South Africa. His early experiences transformed him into a better soldier and provided him with valuable knowledge about leadership in general and the men whom he was charged with leading. Whereas in 1900, his extensive connections with the upper-echelons of society set him apart from his contemporaries, in 1914, it was his status as a veteran of Canada's most recent war that distinguished him from many, but certainly not all, of his fellow soldiers. Now that some of the groundwork has been laid, investigating his accomplishments, character and personality during the First World War will undoubtedly reveal just how influential his time in South Africa truly was.

Everyone, it would seem, learned from their mistakes on the veldt and strove to become better soldiers and better leaders. As Lieutenant-Colonel Steele once reported to Lord Strathcona:

> The men are in good spirits and admirable in their conduct, of which I am sure your lordship will be glad. The fighting has been as heavy as any in the war. Great experience has saved the troops from heavy losses such as took place at other times during the war.[196]

When called upon again to lead men into battle, Agar Adamson was no doubt thankful for his earlier opportunities. He had already learned many costly lessons about leadership and thus was somewhat more ready than his brother officers to face the uncertainties and difficulties that awaited them all. For that, his subordinates were undoubtedly grateful.

Endnotes

1 George Edmund Stevenson Salt, Thomas A. Salt, ed., *Letters and Diary of Lieutenant G.E.S. Salt during the War in South Africa, 1899-1900* (London: John Murray, 1902), 13 Mar 1900, 113.

2 Agar Adamson, Norm Christie, ed., *Letters of Agar Adamson, 1914 to 1919* (Nepean: CEF Books, 1997), Agar Adamson to Mabel Adamson, 4 Mar 1917, 268.

3 Sir George Perley, Minister of the Overseas Military Forces of Canada, held similar views for he too believed that the experienced should be promoted ahead of those who had spent little or no meaningful time at the front. See S.J. Harris, *Canadian Brass: The Making of a Professional*

Army, 1860-1939 (Toronto: University of Toronto Press [UTP], 1988), 125-28. Even before the conclusion of the war in South Africa, some commentators on the state of affairs within the British Army were arguing for the adoption of a promotional system based solely on merit. One proponent, for example, argued that commissions should only be given "through the ranks to men of proved capacity" and that junior officers should be subjected "to searching practical examinations before promotion. In this way commissions would be open to the whole army, and a capacity to handle men, combined with intelligence and industry, would be the only qualifications required." See Sir Reginald Rankin, A *Subaltern's Letters to his Wife* (London: Longmans, Green and Co., 1901), 64-5.

4   Adamson would later find that he had no other option but to place the inexperienced in command. Replacing casualties with qualified and competent leaders was a luxury that he could not always afford. He once wrote, "We are also very short of good senior N.C.O.s having lost so many at Passchendaele and having to fill their places with inexperienced youngsters who do not know the job, either in or out of the line." See Adamson, *Letters*, Agar to Mabel, 21 Jan 1918, 331.

5   For instance, see Ibid., 11 May 1917, 280, where Agar refused to allow his battalion to become "a training school for the convenience of staff officers." In this regard specifically, he prevented Talbot Mercer Papineau from using the PPCLI for his own ends, namely, to increase his chances of success in postwar public life by adding wartime service to his credentials. Adamson only allowed Papineau to join the battalion if he intended to stay the course, rather than join for a short while and then seek safer employment elsewhere; he was eventually killed at Passchendaele. In addition, see Ibid., 9 Jan 1917, 252, where he writes, "I have twenty commissions to suggest today and find it very difficult to choose. The Company Commanders are poor judges and I am worse. It is so hard to hit a line to go on. I have decided to go on guts and not gamble manners so we will probably have some queer fish but the side will be the stronger for it." Because of high casualty rates and Adamson's preferred policy of promoting the experienced, the officer ranks of the PPCLI were soon filled with men who had begun their military careers at the lowest levels. See Ibid., 17 Dec 1917, 327, where he states, "I am making from the Ranks and sending to England, 12 Commissions. It is most difficult deciding as one must not be guided by old prejudices and yet there are limits

I feel. I would like a little new blood in the Regiment, we are now almost entirely composed of men from the Ranks and am looking out for about five."

6   Alexander Reford, "Smith, Donald Alexander, 1st Baron Strathcona and Mount Royal," in Ramsay Cook, ed., *Dictionary of Canadian Biography* [*DCB*], Vol. XIV (Toronto: UTP, 1998), 939-47. See also, Beckles Wilson, *The Life of Lord Strathcona and Mount Royal* (London: Cassell, 1915). As a point of note, Strathcona's Horse did not receive the appellation "Lord" until 1911.

7   Sir Charles G.D. Roberts and Arthur L. Tunnell, *Canadian Who was Who – Volume II – 1875-1937 – A Standard Dictionary of Canadian Biography* (Toronto: Trans-Canada Press, 1938), 1-2, and, Henry James Morgan, ed., *The Canadian Men and Women of the Time: A Hand-Book of Canadian Biography of Living Characters* (Toronto: William Briggs, 1912), 7. For a brief biography of Agar's father, see W.L. Morton, "Adamson, William Agar," in Francess G. Halpenny, ed., *DCB*, Vol. IX (Toronto: UTP, 1976), 4-5.

8   Governor General's Foot Guards, Nominal Rolls, 1886-1896 and 1896-1908, Vol. 11 and Vol. 12, respectively, II-F-6, Record Group [RG] 9, Library and Archives Canada [LAC].

9   Edward Clouston to Lord Strathcona, 18 Apr 1900, File 1, Vol. 2, Manuscript Group [MG] 30 – E166, Lord Strathcona's Horse [LdSH] fonds, LAC. Agar and his wife Mabel must have been on very friendly terms with the Huttons. When in South Africa, Agar was glad that Mabel had paid a visit to Mrs. Hutton. He lamented, "[I] should like to call on General Hutton but he is too far away and a bit engaged." See Agar to Mabel, 2 Aug 1900, Agar Stewart Allan Masterton Adamson fonds, MG 30 – E149, LAC. Frederick Borden, the Minister of Militia and Defence, disagreed with Hutton over several matters of policy and administration and, in Jan 1900, the Laurier government demanded the latter's removal on the grounds of insubordination. At the direction of the Colonial Office, the War Office recalled Hutton; he was later sent to serve with the army then in South Africa.

10   Lord Minto to Strathcona, 18 Apr 1900, File 1, Vol. 2, LdSH fonds, LAC; Desmond Morton, *A Military History of Canada*, 4th ed. (Toronto: McClelland & Stewart, 1999), 113.

11   Sandra Gwyn, *The Private Capital: Ambition and Love in the Age of*

Macdonald and Laurier (Toronto: McClelland & Stewart, 1984), 345. Lord Dufferin served as Canada's Governor General between 1872 and 1878; Lord Ava once held a commission in the 17th Lancers and was killed whilst serving as a war correspondent in South Africa.

12 Agar to Mabel, 27 May 1900, Adamson fonds, LAC.

13 Morton, *Military History*, 96.

14 Ibid., 95. See also, Andrew Greenhill, Cameron Pulsifer, ed., "Narrative of the Volunteer Camp at Niagara, June 1871," *Canadian Military History* 12, 4 (2003), 37-54.

15 Patrick H. Brennan, "Good Men for a Hard Job: Infantry Battalion Commanders in the Canadian Expeditionary Force," *The Canadian Army Journal*, 9.1 (Spring 2006), 13.

16 The Cawthras were colloquially known as "'The Astors of Canada.'" See Gwyn, *Private Capital*, 347. Incidentally, Mabel's cousin, William Mulock, was Canada's Postmaster-General at the turn-of-the-century. See Ibid., 350.

17 "Stately Fall Wedding," 1, 15 Nov 1899, *The Evening Star*.

18 Adamson's biographer has also offered comment on his stature, character and personality. As Sandra Gwyn observes, Agar "was gifted with enormous charm, a man's man who got on splendidly with women." In addition, "For a decade, he'd been one of the most popular young bucks in the capital." All in all, Adamson was a "'classic Edwardian.'" See Gwyn, *Private Capital*, 344-45.

Halifax

19 Carman Miller, *Painting the Map Red: Canada and the South African War, 1899-1902* (Montreal & Kingston: McGill-Queen's University Press, 1993), 145 and 439.

20 Agar to Mabel, 3 Mar 1900, Adamson fonds, LAC. Adamson's remarks on the vices and virtues of Halifax were certainly in keeping with the views of other commentators. As one historian has noted, "nineteenth-century observers found the city to be dirty, dilapidated and dull. They were most scathing about the low-life districts. Few visitors were favourably impressed with the area immediately beneath the Citadel inhabited by the flotsam and jetsam of society. Its street life of prostitutes, drunks and beggars frequently elicited comment." See Judith Fingard,

The Dark Side of Life in Victorian Halifax (Nova Scotia: Pottersfield Press, 1989), 15.

21 For evidence of these and other problems, see "Offer of Militia for Garrison Duty Accepted," 1, 3 Mar 1900; "Making up Militia Garrison for Halifax," 1, 3 Mar 1900; "New Garrison Coming at Once," 1, 6 Mar 1900; "It Will Not be a Picnic For Them," 5, 22 Mar 1900; "Men Are Not Turning Up," 7, 22 Mar 1900; "Youthful Soldiers to Care for Halifax," 5, 23 Mar 1900; "The Officers Quarters at Wellington Barracks," 6, 23 Mar 1900; "Provisional Regiment," 5, 26 Mar 1900; "Another Hitch," 7, 27 Mar 1900; "Provisional Battalion," 2, 30 Mar 1900; "Canadians 780 Strong," 8, 30 Mar 1900; "Refused to Drill," 6, 31 Mar 1900; "Provisional Regiment," 8, 2 Apr 1900; "The Men Don't Like the Orders," 5, 5 Apr 1900; and, "First Death in Regiment," 1, 9 Apr 1900, all *Halifax Herald*.

22 "No Friction in Garrison," 2, 13 Apr 1900, *Morning Chronicle*.

23 "Provisional Regiment," 11, 7 Apr 1900, *Halifax Herald*.

24 "A Grumble from Halifax," 6, 9 Apr 1900, Ibid.

25 Agar to Mabel, 10 Apr 1900, Adamson fonds, LAC.

26 Fingard, *Victorian Halifax*, 16.

27 "A Hearty Send Off," 5, 21 Apr 1900, *Morning Chronicle*. Captain W.S. Conger, from the 15th Battalion, Belleville, was appointed as a lieutenant in 3 RCRI to replace Adamson in the Halifax Garrison. See "Succeeds Capt. Adamson," 7, 25 Apr 1900, *Ottawa Evening Journal*. See also, "Appointed to Halifax," 1, 24 Apr 1900, *Halifax Herald*.

Strathcona's Horse

28 Strathcona to Sir Wilfrid Laurier, 19 Jan 1900, File 3, Vol.1, LdSH fonds, LAC.

29 Ibid. Strathcona also intended that "the officers were to be experienced in life on the plains and in the mountains." See Department of Militia and Defence for the Dominion of Canada, Sessional Paper 35a, *Organization, Equipment, Despatch and Service of the Canadian Contingents during the War in South Africa, 1899-1900* (Ottawa: S.E. Dawson, 1901), 159.

30 Details pertaining to the raising of the SH proper can be found in Militia Orders, No. 26, 1 Feb 1900, File 3, Vol. 4, LdSH fonds, LAC.

31 Kyle McIntyre, "'Sons of good Western stock:' The South African War Artifacts of Private Alexander W. Stewart, Stathcona's Horse,"

Canadian Military History 6, 1 (1997), 87. For a brief description of the time that the original Strathconas spent in Ottawa, see 9/357 to 13/353, MG 30 – E357, Robert Rooke fonds, LAC.

32   Details pertaining to the raising of the SH draft can be found in Militia Orders, No. 92, 23 Apr 1900, File 3, Vol. 4, LdSH fonds, LAC.

33   Strathcona to Department of Militia and Defence, 20 Feb 1900, File 5, Vol. 1, LdSH fonds, LAC. In much the same manner, "War Office suggest I should send out fifty men and one subaltern with personal and horse equipment but without horses to Cape [to] replace possible vacancies [in] my force." See Strathcona to Clouston, 5 Mar 1900, File 10, Vol. 1, Ibid.

34   Carman Miller, "Borden, Sir Frederick William," in Ramsay Cook, ed., *DCB*, Vol. XIV (Toronto: UTP, 1998), 97-101.

35   Strathcona to F.W. Borden, n.d., File 11, Vol. 1, LdSH fonds, LAC.

36   Strathcona to Clouston, n.d., Ibid.

37   Clouston to Strathcona, n.d., Ibid.

38   Borden to Strathcona (Telegram), 16 Apr 1900, File 1, Vol. 2, Ibid., and, Borden to Strathcona (Letter), 16 Apr 1900, Ibid.

39   For example, seven men "out of a long list of applicants" were taken-on-strength at Winnipeg. See "Recruiting in the West," 5, 24 Apr 1900, *Ottawa Free Press*. Adamson later informed Strathcona that the draft was composed of "8 men from Vancouver, 4 from Revelstoke, 18 from Calgary ... 9 from Winnipeg, 4 from Ottawa and 1 from Montreal." See Adamson to Strathcona, 8 Jun 1900, File 3, Vol. 2, LdSH fonds, LAC. A list of the men from Ottawa who joined the draft, along with a brief description of their social standing, can be found in "Off to the War," 8, 1 May 1900, *Ottawa Evening Journal*.

40   Newspaper clipping, "Strickland's Command," 14 Apr 1900, File 1, Vol. 2, LdSH fonds, LAC.

41   "Hundreds of Recruits Offered," 8, 26 Apr 1900, *Ottawa Evening Journal*.

42   For an application received by Strathcona for a commission in the draft, see Unknown to Strathcona, 12 Apr 1900, File 11, Vol. 1, LdSH fonds, LAC.

43   Mabel to Strathcona, 17 Apr 1900, File 1, Vol. 2, Ibid. That Agar was an ambitious young socialite is clear, but how much his wife encouraged him to seek advancement is unknown. He certainly relied on her connections and networks, but she may have unilaterally cultivated them

on his behalf as well. In one of his letters home from Halifax, he wrote: "Of *your* want for husband to get a commission you must be punctual to dinners, do try it is so much more satisfactory. I am still of the opinion that any hour before eight for dinner is too early, absurd and always a rush." See Agar to Mabel, 3 Mar 1900, Adamson fonds, LAC. Italics added by present author. More than a year later, while seeking employment in another contingent bound for South Africa, he penned: "The whole tenor of the letter – and I only received the one of the 18th – seemed to be a desire to bundle me off to South Africa in any capacity and in any event a separation of [at] least six months ... backed up by the warning not to too openly press for a commission...." See Agar to Mabel, 27 Dec 1901, Ibid. Of course, two single references such as these do not prove conclusively that Mabel was the driving force behind Agar's ambition, although it is an intriguing possibility that certainly deserves more thought. It is exceedingly unfortunate that her correspondence to Agar has not survived. This line of thought is not totally unsubstantiated for Sandra Gwyn notes that Mabel once flirted with Minister Borden in order to obtain a commission for her husband. See Gwyn, *Private Capital*, 473, 422 and 328.

44   Clouston wrote to Strathcona, "DONT KNOW HIM PERSONALLY BUT IS WELL RECOMMENDED WAS ON GENERAL HUTTONS STAFF AT AUTUMN MANOEUVERS SHOULD CONSIDER HIM SUITABLE." See Clouston to Strathcona, 18 Apr 1900, File 1, Vol. 2, LdSH fonds, LAC.

45   Borden to Strathcona, 18 Apr 1900, Ibid.

46   Minto to Strathcona, 18 Apr 1900, Ibid.

47   Strathcona to Borden, 19 Apr 1900, Ibid.

48   Strathcona to Minto, 19 Apr 1900, Ibid.

49   Sessional Paper 35a, 159. Adamson's commission as a temporary lieutenant in SH dated from 12 May 1900. See Ibid., 158. Another document, however, has his commission being gazetted on 11 May 1900. See Under Secretary of State for War to Strathcona, 31 May 1900, File 5, Vol. 3, LdSH fonds, LAC. While the prominence of Adamson's patrons and the machinations of his wife surely influenced the awarding of his commission, the possibility also exists that he benefited from mere circumstance. In March 1900, Borden decided that soldiers from the Halifax garrison would be considered first, if and when additional men were required to fill vacancies in the contingents already overseas, namely the Royal Canadian Regiment of

Infantry and the Canadian Mounted Rifles. In fact, "Those joining the Halifax regiment ... have the first chance of seeing service should any vacancies occur." See "Will Get First Chance," 5, 26 Mar 1900, *Halifax Herald*, and, "Impressions of Halifax," 6, 18 Apr 1900, Ibid. If this decision had indeed set the precedent, then volunteers from Halifax would logically have been considered first when it was eventually decided to raise a draft for SH. Considering the apparent lack of competent, qualified and first-rate officers then serving in the garrison, Adamson must have been well-placed to take advantage of this fortuitous situation. With this being said, however, the weight added to his petition by his supporters can neither be dismissed nor overlooked, especially in this era of patronage-driven politics.

50   Gwyn, *Private Capital*, 349.

51   "News of the Canadian," 6, 26 Apr 1900, *Ottawa Free Press*. The main body of Strathcona's Horse was likewise billeted in Ottawa (during the months of February and March 1900) prior to their departure for South Africa.

52   "News of the Canadians," 7, 24 Apr 1900, Ibid. As the same newspaper later observed, "The men were immediately taken out to Lansdowne park, where they went into quarters under supervision of Lt.-Col. Cotton, commandant of the Ottawa Brigade." In addition, "The men arrived in their western dress, but today the department will provide them with a full and complete kit, and the work will be rushed as fast as possible." See "News of the Canadian," 6, 26 Apr 1900, Ibid. Another newspaper similarly observed, "They will be outfitted and equipped here without delay...." See "Arrive Tomorrow," 7, 24 Apr 1900, *Ottawa Evening Journal*. A list of stores issued to the draft in Ottawa can be found in Sessional Paper 35a, 21. Unlike the regiment proper, the draft took no horses.

53   For Lord Minto's accounts of the fire, see Paul Stevens and John T. Saywell, eds., *Lord Minto's Canadian Papers: A Selection of the Public and Private Papers of the Fourth Earl of Minto, 1898-1904*, Vol. I (Toronto: The Champlain Society, 1981), 346-47 and 349-51. Ottawa newspapers dating from the time of the conflagration also offer considerable detail, as might be expected.

54   "George Sparks is Going," 1, 28 Apr 1900, *Ottawa Free Press*.

55   Narrative, 2, MG 29 – E20, Thomas Easton Howell fonds, LAC.

56   "George Sparks is Going," 1, 28 Apr 1900, *Ottawa Free Press*.

57   When at church, for instance, the men of the draft took up a "special

collection" on behalf of the victims of the late fire. See "Strathconas at Church," 5, 28 Apr 1900, *Ottawa Evening Journal*.

58   "Off to the Wars," 3, 1 May 1900, *Ottawa Free Press*.

59   "Mounted Policemen," 5, 1 May 1900, *Ottawa Evening Journal*.

60   "Strathcona Recruits," 7, 1 May 1900, *Montreal Daily Star*.

61   In the opinion of one newspaper, "The men looked trim and neat in the khaki uniforms, with broad-brimmed hats." See "Off to the War," 8, 1 May 1900, *Ottawa Evening Journal*.

62   Vol. 30, II-A-3, RG 9, LAC. The small group of men who possessed military experience included William Bartram (43rd Battalion, Canadian Militia), David Burnet (2nd Montreal Regiment, Canadian Artillery), Robert B. Heron (13th Field Battery, Canadian Artillery), Colin William McMillan ('B' Squadron, Manitoba Dragoons, Canadian Militia) and Cecil Morris (90th Battalion, Canadian Militia). The draft also included Agar's good friend, George Sparkes of the Interior Department, who was one of the last recruits to be attested (as an orderly to Adamson) and who will "be missed in the Capital particularly in social circles, where he was justly popular." Sparkes "will be the only man in the detachment wearing a medal, having served in the North West rebellion." See "George Sparks is Going," 1, 28 Apr 1900, *Ottawa Free Press*. During the Rebellion, Sparkes served as a private with the Ottawa Sharpshooters. See Barbara M. Wilson, *Military General Service, 1793-1814 (Canadian Recipients) – Egypt Medal, 1882-1889 (Canadian Recipients) – North West Canada, 1885* (London: Spink & Son Ltd., 1975), 167. As Strathcona wished, all the men of the draft were single. Adamson later learned on his voyage to South Africa that his Sergeant-Major was the son of an Irish landlord, one Colonel Buchanan. See Agar to Mabel, 27 May 1900, Adamson fonds, LAC. Additionally, two men belonging to the draft had served with Adamson in the provisional battalion. As they were militiamen and had only served in Halifax for a brief period, they could not have had a great deal of experience, but considering the credentials of other individuals with whom they were now associated, they at least had some. See "City News in Brief," 2, 28 Apr 1900, *Halifax Herald*.

63   Diary entry for 5 May 1900, David Morrison Stewart Collection, *Canadian Letters and Images Project* [CLIP]. Online collection available at: http://web.mala.bc.ca/davies/Letters.Images/homepage.htm.

64   Adamson to Strathcona, 8 Jun 1900, File 3, Vol. 2, LdSH fonds, *LAC*.

Lieutenant Salt of the 1st Battalion, Royal Welch Fusiliers, also used the time aboard ship to advantage. As he recalled, "We give the men as much exercise as is possible on board ship, having daily parades for physical drill and doubling round the deck." See Salt, *Letters and Diary*, 27 Oct 1899, 6. See also, Ibid., 1 Nov 1899, 8.

65   Diary entry for 23 Apr 1900, MG 29 – E50, Robert Burns Heron fonds, *LAC*.

66   Diary entry for 8 May 1900, Stewart Collection, *CLIP*. Stewart seems to have made an error when spelling the surname Adamson. The early entries in his diary record the name Anderson, although the spelling is later corrected. Stewart is recorded in the nominal roll as a member of the draft, so the officer to whom he was referring was Adamson who was in command.

67   Newspaper Clipping "Farewell to Strathcona's Men," 11 May 1900, Scrapbook, MG 30 – E83, John Edwards Leckie fonds, *LAC*, and, Newspaper Clipping, "Strathcona Horse," 11 May 1900, Ibid. As Heron recalls: "When he appeared we gave him three rousing cheers. He in turn have us a short address and a hand shake all round." See diary entry for 23 Apr 1900, Heron fonds, *LAC*.

68   Ibid.

69   Diary entry for 18 May 1900, Ibid.

70   Agar to Mabel, 27 May 1900, Adamson fonds, *LAC*.

71   Ibid.

72   Adamson to Strathcona, 8 Jun 1900, File 3, Vol. 2, LdSH fonds, *LAC*.

73   Ibid.

74   Ibid. Agar was apparently quite anxious to join the fray. After outlining the accomplishments of the draft, he again remarked, "I sincerely trust they will give us a chance to do ourselves credit." See Ibid.

South Africa

75   For confirmation, see diary entry for 10 Jun 1900, Heron fonds, *LAC*. Before describing Adamson's brief, if interesting, career in South Africa, it must be made clear that not every action in which he was engaged will be examined. In many instances, he is not at all mentioned in the historical record concerning these events, and thus his participation remains circumstantial and can only be inferred. Because he is not mentioned by

name, any assessment of his leadership abilities during specific engagements would be based solely on speculation and could only be inferred by the relative success or failure of the SH as a whole. Owing to these circumstances then, only those engagements for which evidence exists concerning Adamson's involvement will be treated herein.

76   Agar to Mabel, 3 Jun 1900, Adamson fonds, *LAC*.

77   For a brief description of the proposed attack, see Miller, *Painting the Map Red*, 309-11.

78   Agar to Mabel, 3 Jun 1900, Adamson fonds, *LAC*.

79   Diary entry for 2 Jun 1900, Stewart Collection, *CLIP*. The references to Adamson as a captain are not in error, even though he was obliged to serve in South Africa as a lieutenant, for at this time he was still wearing the badges indicative of the former rank. Once he joined the SH proper, he removed his superfluous pip and assumed his position as a subaltern.

80   The provision of free alcohol to his men was something that seems to have become a standard practice for Adamson for he resorted to it again during the First World War. See Adamson, *Letters*, Agar to Mabel, 5 Nov 1915, 98-99.

81   Agar to Mabel, 9 Jun 1900, Adamson fonds, *LAC*.

82   Other officers experienced similar feelings. While serving with the 1st Battalion, Royal Welch Fusiliers, Lieutenant G.E.S. Salt wrote, "I am in charge of the maxim gun, – rather an anxious job, as it is not an easy thing to work well, and one feels responsible if anything goes wrong." See Salt, *Letters and Diary*, 21 Nov 1899, 18.

83   Rankin, *Subaltern's Letters*, 77.

84   Agar to Mabel, 9 Jun 1900, Adamson fonds, *LAC*.

85   The experiences of the SH with the Natal Field Force are beyond the scope of this present work. Interested readers are instead encouraged to see Miller, *Painting the Map Red*, Chapters 21 and 22, 309-339.

86   Narrative, 3, Howell fonds, *LAC*.

87   Diary entry for 21 Jun 1900, Stewart Collection, *CLIP*.

88   Diary entry for 16 Jun 1900, Ibid.

89   Agar to Mabel, 23 Jun 1900, Adamson fonds, *LAC*. William Bartram held two certificates from the Toronto military school and was apparently well connected, being the son of the Surveyor of Customs. See "Strathcona's Horse," 5, 30 Apr 1900, *Ottawa Free Press*. One month earlier, Agar also noted, "My men are all behaving well." Agar was being only

partially truthful on this score as his men were anything but obedient at times. See Agar to Mabel, 27 May 1900, Adamson fonds, *LAC*.

90   Agar to Mabel, 23 Jun 1900, Ibid.

91   Ibid.

92   Ibid.

93   For instance, Stewart recalled, "18 of us with the Cap't went out scouting." See diary entry for 30 Jun 1900, Stewart Collection, *CLIP*.

94   In the same letter, however, Adamson also noted, "With the exception of about six my men are splendid fellows and developing every day." See Agar to Mabel, 3 Jul 1900, Adamson fonds, *LAC*.

95   Ibid. For additional information concerning these acts, see Chris Madsen, "Canadian Troops and Farm Burning in the South African War," *Canadian Military Journal* 6, 2 (Summer 2005), 49-58. Contemporary accounts kept by unit members of the activities performed by Strathcona's Horse frequently make reference to such endeavours. George Alexander Bowers recorded in his diary, for instance, "I think we will have to move camp soon as we have commandeered almost everything eatable about here as well as all the wood, which is a very scarce article;" "Looting orders read this a.m. as it has been getting too common;" "robbed an orchard;" "burned a mill;" and "We had to do a lot of theiv [sic] – commandeering on this trip in order to live." See George Alexander Bowers' diary entries for 19 Dec 1900, 22 Dec 1900, 25 Dec 1900, 28 Dec 1900 and 9 Jan 1901, respectively, M 7908, Robson family fonds, *Glenbow Museum*. See also, for example, diary entries for 26 Jun 1900, 3 Jul 1900, 20 Sep 1900 and 27 Dec 1900, M 1037, Ivor Edward Cecil Rice-Jones fonds, *Glenbow Museum*.

96   For confirmation, see diary entry for 2 Jul 1900, Heron fonds, *LAC*.

97   Agar to Mabel, 5 Jul 1900, Adamson fonds, *LAC*. T.E. Howell admitted shortly after the war, "Many of our fellows had been cowboys and had spent the greater part of their lives riding over the prairie looking for lost cattle or shooting dear and antelope. They had therefore all the qualifications required in scouting on active service and quickly settled down to the work the regiment had to perform." See Narrative, 8, Howell fonds, *LAC*. While this may have been true for riding, it apparently did not apply to purely military matters. The men, despite their western background, still required some time to learn how to fight as mounted infantry. Adamson, then, in this regard specifically, was no different from his soldiers.

98   Agar to Mabel, 5 Jul 1900, Adamson fonds, *LAC*.
99   Steele to Strathcona, Greylingstad, 3 Jul 1900, File 2, Vol. 6, LdSH Fonds, *LAC*.

Canada's Second Victoria Cross of the War – Wolve Spruit

Note: The maps included in the text that illustrate the battle at Wolve Spruit are not drawn to scale, nor are they particularly detailed. The basis for this series of sketches was a hand-drawn map that Agar included in one of his letters to his wife to help her follow the flow of the battle. In much the same manner, the accompanying sketches are offered merely in the hope of demonstrating to the reader the relative position of one unit to another. All of these maps, in addition to the other two that appear in this volume, were kindly drawn by Mr. William Constable.

100 See Agar to Mabel, 5 Jul 1900, Adamson fonds, *LAC*. The quotations appearing in the text above have been taken from this letter.
101 Ibid.
102 Ibid.
103 Narrative, 4-5, Howell fonds, *LAC*.
104 Agar to Mabel, 5 Jul 1900, Adamson fonds, *LAC*. It is possible that Adamson may have been ordered to abandon his distinguishing dress in favour of a more inconspicuous garb. Lieutenant G.E.S. Salt was once ordered to dress "as much as possible like the men" owing to the fact that so many officers had been killed since the beginning of the war. See Salt, *Letters and Diary*, 21 Nov 1899, 16.
105 Narrative, 4, Howell fonds, *LAC*.
106 Agar to Mabel, 3 Jul 1900, Adamson fonds, *LAC*.
107 Newspaper Clipping, "With Strathcona's Horse," Scrapbook, Leckie fonds, *LAC*.
108 Andrew Miller's unpublished 1912 manuscript, 89-92, M 3608, Lord Strathcona's Horse [LdSH] fonds, *Glenbow Museum*. Unfortunately, a portion of page 90 has been excised from the archival copy of this manuscript, thus forcing the present author to rely upon a partially incomplete account of the action for details.
109 Agar to Mabel, 5 Jul 1900, Adamson fonds, *LAC*.
110 See *London Gazette*, 14 Sep 1900. Nearly two months after the engagement, in Sep, Richardson received word that he had been awarded

the VC. Adamson and the men of SH were understandably excited at the news, so too was their benefactor. As Lieutenant-Colonel Steele later wrote to Strathcona, "Many thanks for your kind message of congratulations to Sergt. Richardson on his being awarded the Victoria Cross! He wishes me to thank you most sincerely for the trouble you have taken to let him know. I may add that the whole regiment are [sic] pleased with the message, and hope that some more of them may yet be so fortunate as to have such an opportunity." See Steele to Strathcona, Spitzkop, 20 Sep 1900, File 3, Vol. 6, LdSH fonds, *LAC*. See also, Miller's unpublished 1912 manuscript, 160, LdSH fonds, *Glenbow Museum*. Additional awards earned by members of SH can be found in *South African War Honours & Awards, 1899-1902: Officers and Men of the Army and Navy Mentioned in Despatches* (London: Arms and Armour Press with Hayward and Hall, 1971).

111 Arthur Bishop, *Our Bravest and Our Best: The Stories of Canada's Victoria Cross Winners* (Toronto: McGraw-Hill Ryerson Ltd., 1995), 18. Some years later, Lucius McCormick recalled with some amusement: "The first Victoria Cross awarded to Canadians in the Boer War was won by Sergeant Richardson of Lord Strathcona's Horse, who on board ship had pulled an aching back-tooth for me with a pair of horse forceps." See Memoirs, 50, MG 30 – E396, Lucius McCormick fonds, *LAC*. For additional details regarding Richardson's life, both before and after the South African War, see Bishop, *Our Bravest and Our Best*, 18.

112 Private Alex McArthur and Private G.A.S. Sparkes were both wounded, while Private C.J. Isbester, Private J.C. McDougall and Sergeant A. Stringer were listed as missing after the action. See Casualty Return, n.d., File 2, Vol. 6, LdSH fonds, *LAC*. All of these individuals belonged to the draft that Adamson took to South Africa and were either captured or wounded in their very first engagement. This was certainly not the type of experience that they had anticipated or looked forward too. A brief account of the action is provided in "Modest, Brave Chap," 12, 27 Nov 1900, *Montreal Daily Star*, and repeated in, "Brave Arthur Richardson," 22, 28 Nov 1900, *Family Herald and Weekly Star*. Robert Rooke also offers an account of this action in his memoirs. See 45/321 to 46/320, Rooke fonds, *LAC*. The accuracy of this account may be suspect owing to the fact that he himself was not engaged with Adamson's troop, so the version of events that he relates was obviously told to him later; he

was also writing (apparently) after the First World War, some twenty years after the event occurred.

113   Agar to Mabel, 5 Jul 1900, Adamson fonds, *LAC*.

Agar's Remaining Time in South Africa

114   A return indicating the names of the individuals who died while on active service with SH, along with the squadron to which they belonged, can be found in File 13, Vol. 5, LdSH fonds, *LAC*. Similarly, for a casualty summary that lists such categories as the strength of the SH upon arrival in South Africa, the total number killed, whether by action or by disease, the number invalided home, the number appointed to commissions in the British Army, etc., see File 19, Vol. 2, Ibid. See also, document dated S.S. Lake Erie, 14 Feb 1901, File 2, Vol. 3, Ibid.

115   Diary entry for 14 Jul 1900, Heron fonds, *LAC*. It is also possible, of course, that his reluctance to pursue the enemy may also have resulted from the fact that he had already tasted battle, the excitement, confusion and cost of which was now familiar to him, and thus his curiosity may have been dampened. He also knew how he would react under sustained fire and thus his personal need to learn about his steadiness had probably been satisfied.

116   Agar to Mabel, 10 Jul 1900, Adamson fonds, *LAC*.

117   Ibid.

118   Ibid.

119   Agar to Mabel, 12 Jul 1900, Ibid.

120   Ibid.

121   Agar to Mabel, 15 Jul 1900, Ibid. Speaking about SH as a whole, T.E. Howell, who came to South African with Adamson and the draft, later recalled, "As in all colonial corps the discipline in Strathcona's Horse was not as strict and rigid as that enforced in imperial regiments and our (comparatively) free and easy ways used often I think to horrify the imperial officers and soldiers." See Narrative, 6, Howell fonds, *LAC*. Adamson certainly demanded a high degree of discipline from his soldiers, and in this regard, he may have been emulating many of his British counterparts. There are no references in his letters of allowing a crime to go unpunished (except looting). To be sure, when he mentions crime at all, it is only to demonstrate how he punished the perpetrator. Of course, he may have

overlooked petty infractions, but he did not make these actions known to posterity.

122 Bowers' diary entry for 18 Jul 1900, Robson family fonds, *Glenbow Museum*.

123 S.B. Steele, *Forty Years in Canada* (Toronto: McClelland, Goodchild & Stewart, 1914), 346. Steele also wrote, "I am very well pleased with the draft sent out, and with the horses brought up with them." See Steele to Strathcona, Leeuw Spruit, 20 Jul 1900, File 2, Vol. 6, LdSH fonds, *LAC*.

124 Steele to Strathcona, Paarde Kop, 5 Aug 1900, Ibid.

125 Agar to Mabel, 23 Jul 1900, Adamson fonds, *LAC*.

126 Diary entry for 6 Aug 1900, Stewart Collection, *CLIP*. A later history of the Strathconas' time in South Africa suggests that the draft was immediately divided amongst the under-strength troops of the regiment, although this is in error. As related therein, "When the draft joined the regiment at Waterval, the vacancies in the ranks from casualties were filled, and the corps brought up to its original strength in men and horses." See Miller's unpublished 1912 manuscript, 91-2, LdSH fonds, *Glenbow Museum*. The draft was kept as a separate command under Adamson until it was disbanded in August.

127 Agar to Mabel, 15 Aug 1900, Adamson fonds, *LAC*.

128 Agar to Mabel, 2 Aug 1900, Ibid. See also, diary entries for 23 Jul 1900, 27 Jul 1900, 29 Jul 1900, 30 Jul 1900 and 31 Jul 1900, Stewart Collection, *CLIP*, in which it is recorded that the draft, prior to being disbanded, did a lot of "scouting" and acting as the "advance guard" to the main body of Strathconas or the column in which they were serving.

129 McIntyre, "South African War Artifacts," 89.

130 Agar to Mabel, 15 Aug 1900, Adamson fonds, *LAC*.

131 Sessional Paper 35a, 165.

132 Steele to Strathcona, Tweyfreaar Court, 16 Aug 1900, File 2, Vol. 6, LdSH fonds, *LAC*. Recalling the action, T.E. Howell wrote, "Some resistance was offered and a ridge of hills in front of the town had to be shelled by the big guns. ... At dusk when the order came to enter the town the hitherto orderly advance of Strathcona's Horse changed into a wild race to see who would get in first." See Narrative, 9, Howell fonds, *LAC*.

133 Agar to Mabel, 15 Aug 1900, Adamson fonds, *LAC*. As Steele recalled, "One squadron under orders from Lord Dundonald was sent forward to seize Ermelo, if possible. This was done. The telegraph and other

public offices were taken possession of and posts established in the town." See Steele to Strathcona, Tweyfreaar Court, 16 Aug 1900, File 2, Vol. 6, LdSH fonds, *LAC*. T.E. Howell mentions that Ermelo was occupied "without opposition" after SH had endured "a long and painful march through a blinding dust storm." See Narrative, 10, Howell fonds, *LAC*.

134   Agar to Mabel, 15 Aug 1900, Adamson fonds, *LAC*. For comments pertaining to Carolina, see Steele to Strathcona, Tweyfreaar Court, 16 Aug 1900, File 2, Vol. 6, LdSH fonds, *LAC*.

135   Narrative, 13, Howell fonds, *LAC*. For a brief account of the capture of Machadodorp, see Miller's unpublished 1912 manuscript, 117-18, LdSH fonds, *Glenbow Museum*, and, Steele to Strathcona, Badfontein, 3 Sep 1900, File 2, Vol. 6, LdSH fonds, *LAC*. Unfortunately, Adamson is mentioned in neither account.

136   Miller's unpublished 1912 manuscript, 125-26, LdSH fonds, *Glenbow Museum*. The action at Crocodile River was not a total loss, for Steele observed after the war, "Before going into camp the country to the front was scouted and valuable information gained." See Sessional Paper 35a, 167. Immediately after the action, he recalled, "We came in contact with the enemy at Crocodile river. The Pom Pom was brought up and the Boers pressed back. We halted here for the night to enable the rest of the army to catch up. During the day the flankers of the corps captured several prisoners and gained valuable information regarding the enemy's movements which has since proven correct." See Steele to Strathcona, Badfontein, 3 Sep 1900, File 2, Vol. 6, LdSH fonds, *LAC*.

137   Agar to Mabel, 22 Mar 1901, Adamson fonds, *LAC*.

138   A very detailed account of the engagement at Crocodile Valley can be found in Narrative, 14-7, Howell fonds, *LAC*. According to Howell's account, MacGillivray did not leave the other soldiers to go searching for chickens, but rather to engage a sniper that was offering harassing fire. Whatever his motivations, he removed himself from Adamson's control with the aforementioned result.

139   Ibid., 16.

140   In late-October, after the Natal Field Force had been disbanded, the SH, along with a number of other units, began chasing the Boer leader General Christiaan de Wet. For an account of these activities, see Miller, *Painting the Map Red*, Chapter 23, 340-357.

141 Additional letters that document some of the activities of SH during its time in South Africa, but which unfortunately do not mention Adamson, include J.C. Walker, "We Have to Do or Die: A Strathcona in South Africa, April 1900," in J.L. Granatstein and Norman Hillmer, eds., *Battle Lines: Eyewitness Accounts from Canada's Military History* (Toronto: Thomas Allen Publishers, 2004), 89, and Charles and Bert Rooke, "Cavalry in South Africa," in Ibid., 90-4. No attempt will therefore be made to assess Agar's leadership during this period for any critique would be purely speculative. Commenting without concrete evidence on his involvement in an accidental shooting that occurred in his troop (see Sessional Paper 35a, 171), on his participation in an alleged lynching of Boer prisoners after they had surrendered (see Miller, *Painting the Map Red*, 323-24) or on his role in a drunken riot at Machadodorp (see Ibid., 338-39) would certainly not be wise and will not be pursued.

142 Strathcona to Steele, 3 Jul 1901, File 5, Vol. 4, LdSH fonds, LAC.

143 Steele to Strathcona, Greylingstad, 25 Jul 1900, File 2, Vol. 6, Ibid.

144 Narrative, 2, Howell fonds, LAC.

145 Agar to Mabel, 2 Aug 1900, Adamson fonds, LAC.

146 As Agar related to Mabel, "I dined with five men of the Buffs;" "Dined with the Queens tonight. Have only 5 of their original officers left, a good lot, did me very well…;" "Lunched with…16th Bengal Lancers;" and, "The Colonel of the Lancasters has very decently asked me to dinner." See Agar to Mabel, 9 Jun 1900, 12 Jul 1900, 15 Jul 1900, and, 3 Aug 1900, respectively, Ibid. Adamson also enjoyed their company on board the *Assaye* as well. Later in the war when serving as a captain with the 6th Canadian Mounted Rifles (see later text above), Agar declined to join the mess of a British regiment owing to the cost that would be entailed. He was no doubt disappointed as he surely would have felt quite at home and at ease. See Agar to Mabel, 20 Jul 1902, Ibid. Adamson's experience on this point was not entirely unique as one commentator observed, "The curse of our present army system is the halo of social effulgence which encircles the officers' mess. Unless a boy has money of his own he cannot go into the 'smart' regiments, for two reasons; the pay is too low, and the standard of living is too high." See Rankin, *Subaltern's Letters*, 65.

147 Carman Miller, "The Unhappy Warriors: Conflict and Nationality among the Canadian Troops during the South African War," *Journal of Imperial and Commonwealth History* 23, 1 (1995), 99.

148 Agar to Mabel, 23 Jul 1900, Adamson fonds, *LAC*.
149 Agar to Mabel, 15 Aug 1900, Ibid.
150 Agar to Mabel, 2 Aug 1900, Ibid.
151 Agar to Mabel, 23 Jul 1900, Ibid. He also noted, "Steel [sic] is a failure, a good fighter, but selfish, and most inconsiderate to his men." See Agar to Mabel, 2 Aug 1900, Ibid. Others within the regiment apparently disliked him as well, for Adamson later wrote, "Col Steel [sic] most thoroughly hated, it is a great pity." See Agar to Mabel, 15 Aug 1900, Ibid. Whatever his opinions may have been, Agar seems to have kept them to himself, save for his wife, and did not make them public record. For additional comments regarding Steele's behaviour in Halifax upon the return of SH to Canada, see Mr. Taylor to Strathcona, 31 Mar 1901, File 7, Vol. 3, LdSH fonds, *LAC*.
152 Agar to Mabel, 15 Aug 1900, Adamson fonds, *LAC*.
153 Ibid.
154 Agar to Mabel, 5 Mar 1901, Ibid.

Invalided and Recuperation

155 Lieutenant Salt, a contemporary of Adamson and whose letters are cited herein, died of enteric fever on 3 Apr 1900.
156 Bowers' diary entry for 20 Oct 1900, Robson family fonds, *Glenbow Museum*.
157 Steele to Strathcona, Frederichstad, 4 Nov 1900, File 3, Vol. 6, LdSH fonds, *LAC*. In September, Leckie noted while at Spitz Kop that "Seven of our officers are down with fever." See Leckie to Pater, 17 Sep 1900, Vol. 2, Leckie fonds, *LAC*.
158 Roll of Officers, N.C.O.'s and Men Invalided to England, 1, File 8, Vol. 6, LdSH Fonds, *LAC*. Adamson was officially invalided from "A" Squadron on 28 Nov 1900. On his way to hospital, Agar's baggage was somehow misplaced. As he recorded, "All my baggage has been lost, which means a very serious matter." See Agar to Mabel, 7 Nov 1900, Adamson fonds, *LAC*. According to Gwyn, this unfortunate turn of events, wherein important documents relating to his pay had been lost, forced Adamson to remain in London and negotiate with the WO in an attempt to gain his due compensation.
159 Newspaper Clipping, "Officers Coming Home," Scrapbook, Leckie fonds, *LAC*.

160 "Social and Personal," 5, 15 Jan 1901, *Toronto Daily Star*.
161 "Social and Personal," 5, 25 Feb 1901, Ibid.
162 Adamson to Mr. Colmer, Hotel des Anglais, 20 Jan 1901, File 18, Vol. 2, LdSH fonds, *LAC*.

London

163 Agar noted, "I have to go before a Medical board on Thursday and nothing can be done about pay until they have reported, but it will be all right." See Agar to Mabel, undated although probably 4 Feb 1901, Adamson fonds, LAC. He later reported with some satisfaction, "I went before a Medical Board this morning and they pronounced me sound and will recommend that I be sent to Canada when I feel so disposed." See Agar to Mabel, 7 Mar 1901, Ibid.
164 Agar to Mabel, 17 Mar 1901, Ibid.
165 Agar to Mabel, 18 Mar 1901, Ibid. Also in the way of shopping, Agar related: "I bought an awfully fine old wine cooler, mahogany clamped with brass, it came off H.M.S. Indus which was broken up some years ago." See Agar to Mabel, 20 Mar 1901, Ibid.
166 Agar to Mabel, 16 Mar 1901, Ibid. See also, Agar to Mabel, 22 Mar 1901, Ibid., for another attempted call on Lord Strathcona.
167 Agar to Mabel, 13 Mar 1901, Ibid. The soldier who invited Agar to dinner was Sir Henry Green.
168 Agar to Mabel, 14 Mar 1901, Ibid.
169 For a brief description of Steele's behaviour, see Agar to Mabel, 3 Feb 1901, Ibid. As Adamson later recalled, "I got the full story of Lord Strathcona's lunch at the Savoy." See Agar to Mabel, 5 Mar 1901, Ibid. Other SH officers were not on their best behaviour either, as Adamson was quick to observe. See Agar to Mabel, 22 Mar 1901, Ibid. Seeing that Agar disliked them generally as a lot, these revelations probably confirmed his earlier opinions.

Back in Canada

170 Agar to Mabel, 23 Mar 1901, Ibid.
171 Agar to Mabel, 15 Apr 1901, Ibid. Additional individuals with whom Agar dined included Col. Hubert Foster, the Quarter-Master General, 1898-1901 (see Agar to Mabel, 15 Apr 1901, Ibid.) and Sir

Richard Cartwright (see Agar to Mabel, 31 Oct 1901, Ibid.). For a brief account of Cartwright's life, see Cecilia Morgan and Robert Craig Brown, "Cartwright, Sir Richard John," in Ramsay Cook, ed., *DCB*, Vol. XIV (Toronto: UTP, 1998), 200-05. Agar also had the opportunity to dine "with a Prime Minister last night and played cork pool till midnight. Haultain is the gentleman's name and he is P.M. of the N.W.T. an excellent chap." See Agar to Mabel, 26 Oct 1901, Ibid.

172 Agar to Mabel, 15 Apr 1901, Ibid.

173 Agar to Mabel, 11 Apr 1901, Ibid.

174 For letters relating to these and other activities, see Agar to Mabel, 11 Apr 1901, 20 Apr 1901, 7 Oct 1901, 21 Oct 1901, 22 Oct 1901, 23 Oct 1901 and 6 Dec 1901, Ibid.

175 Agar to Mabel, 6 Apr 1901, Ibid.

South Africa ... again

176 "Paardeberg Anniversary Dinner," 1, 28 Feb 1902, *Globe*.

177 Agar to Mabel, 19 Mar 1901, Adamson fonds, *LAC*. Interestingly, in December 1901, Agar informed his wife, "They offered me a Lieutenant's Commission in the new Contingent well down in the list. I refused it after due and careful consideration of the pros and cons." See Agar to Mabel, 9 Dec 1901, Ibid. Although Mabel was expecting their first child at the time, Agar seemed more concerned about the quality and character of the men that he would be forced to serve with. As he noted in a private letter, "I wired you yesterday concerning the Contingent, it is too long a subject to discuss, but under the present circumstances, and considering the lot of cads with commissions, it is only under exceptional circumstances that I should think of going." See Agar to Mabel, 22 Dec 1901, Ibid. While Agar was certainly ambitious and eager to see active service again, it seems clear that he only wanted to serve with those soldiers whom *he* found acceptable.

178 Adamson to Borden, 27 Mar 1902, Vol. 21, II-A-3, RG 9, *LAC*.

179 The Colonel to whom Agar referred was in fact Julian Byng who would later command the Canadian Corps for a time during the First World War. Adamson was probably quite pleased to serve under Byng again.

180 Adamson to Lieutenant-Colonel A.L. Jarvis, 5 Apr 1902, Vol. 21, II-A-3, RG 9, *LAC*. See also, Adamson to Jarvis, 5 Apr 1902, Vol. 22,

Ibid. For a letter relating to Adamson's equitation board, see Agar to Mabel, 26 Oct 1901, Adamson fonds, *LAC*.

181   "Parties Recommended and those Recommending," 1 Apr 1902, Vol. 23, II-A-3, RG 9, *LAC*.

182   Agar's dislike of Steele can be glimpsed in Gwyn, *Private Capital*, 361-64.

183   In early-1902, at the request of the British government, the Department of Militia and Defence assumed the responsibility of raising a number of additional regiments for service in South Africa. The men so recruited were formed into the 3rd, 4th, 5th and 6th CMR. Since they did not recruit them personally, the COs of each unit met their soldiers as a group for the first time in Halifax. Each unit consisted of approximately 509 soldiers, all ranks, and a conscious effort was made to give a regional character to each regiment and a territorial identity to each squadron therein. See Miller, *Painting the Map Red*, 414-23.

184   Ibid., 418.

185   Ibid., 417. See also, Agar to Mabel, 12 Jun 1902, Adamson fonds, *LAC*, for comments pertaining to the strengths and weaknesses of the officers of 6 CMR.

186   Miller's unpublished 1912 manuscript, 200, LdSH fonds, *Glenbow Museum*.

187   Agar to Mabel, 11 Jun 1902, Adamson fonds, *LAC*.

188   Agar to Mabel, 28 June 1902, Ibid.

189   Agar to Mabel, 12 Jun 1902, Ibid.

190   Ibid.

191   Agar to Mabel, 26 Jul 1902, Ibid. On this occasion, Adamson's stature and political connections failed to work in his advantage. His letter to Mabel, in which he wrote, "I have written to Lord Milner, enclosing H. Ex's [His Excellency's] letter, and asking him to find me a billet," was followed by another a few days later relating that nothing could be done for him. See Agar to Mabel, 28 Jun 1902 and 5 Jul 1902, Ibid.

Concluding Thoughts

192   Adamson, *Letters*, Agar to Mabel, 24 Nov 1917, 317. Also, during the First World War, he wrote, "I am beginning to find out more about the men in the Company sitting about and talking during the day." See Adamson, *Letters*, Agar to Mabel, 24 Mar 1915, 49.

193 See, Ibid., 21 Feb 1916, 149.

194 For instance, see Ibid., 11 May 1917, 280, where Agar refused to allow his battalion to become "a training school for the convenience of staff officers."

195 Ibid., 9 Jan 1917, 252.

196 Steele to Strathcona, Spitzkop, 12 Sep 1900, File 3, Vol. 6, LdSH fonds, *LAC*.

Map and Image Credits

All maps were kindly drawn by Mr. William Constable.

Front Cover Art: Mr. Peter Prince, University of Manitoba.

Image 1: "Ottawa Hockey Team," Unknown, PA-110040, *Library and Archives Canada.*

Image 2: "Agar Adamson costumed as Napoleon Bonaparte, Victorian Era Ball held in Toronto," William James Topley, PA-138384, *Library and Archives Canada.*

Image 3: "Lord Strathcona and Mount Royal," Lafayette, C-3841, *Library and Archives Canada.*

Image 4: "Col. S.B. Steele, Commanding Strathcona's Horse," Steele and Co., C-17553, *Library and Archives Canada.*

Image 5: "Personnel of Strathcona's Horse en route to South Africa aboard S.S. MONTEREY," Unknown, C-171, *Library and Archives Canada.*

Image 6: *Lord Strathcona's Horse (Royal Canadians) Regimental Museum.*

Image 7: "Officers, Strathcona Horse," Henry Dunsford, PA-210511, *Library and Archives Canada.*

Image 8: "Strathcona Camp, Cape Town," Henry Dunsford, PA-28918, *Library and Archives Canada.*

Image 9: *Lord Strathcona's Horse (Royal Canadians) Regimental Museum.*

Image 10: *Lord Strathcona's Horse (Royal Canadians) Regimental Museum.*

Image 11: "Field Hospital at Paardeberg Drift," Reinhold Thiele, C-6097, *Library and Archives Canada.*

Image 12: "Interior of a Ward at a Military Hospital in South Africa," W. Dobbs, PA-124925, *Library and Archives Canada.*

Image 13: "S.S. WINNIFREDIAN Carrying Personnel of the 4th and 6th Canadian Mounted Rifles, H.J. Woodside, PA-16418, *Library and Archives Canada.*

Image 14: "5th Canadian Mounted Rifles in camp at Durban," H.J. Woodside, PA-16431, *Library and Archives Canada.*

Image 15: "Lieutenant-Colonel Agar Adamson," *Princess Patricia's Canadian Light Infantry Regimental Museum and Archives.*

Image 16: "Christmas dinner including Captain Agar Adamson of Princess Patricia's Canadian Light Infantry," A.S.A.M. Adamson, PA-139711, *Library and Archives Canada.*

Back Cover: "Return of Lord Strathcona's Horse from South Africa," Arden & Archer, PA-181427, *Library and Archives Canada.*

Select Bibliography

NOTE: The following is merely a list of those sources that the interested reader may wish to pursue; it is not a comprehensive list of all material used in the preparation of this volume.

Adamson, Agar. Norm Christie, ed. *Letters of Agar Adamson, 1914 to 1919*. Nepean: CEF Books, 1997.

Bishop, Arthur. *Our Bravest and Our Best: The Stories of Canada's Victoria Cross Winners*. Toronto: McGraw-Hill Ryerson Limited, 1995.

Department of Militia and Defence for the Dominion of Canada. *Organization, Equipment, Despatch and Service of the Canadian Contingents during the War in South Africa, 1899-1900*. Sessional Paper 35a. Ottawa: S.E. Dawson, 1901.

Granatstein, J.L. and Norman Hillmer, eds. *Battle Lines: Eyewitness Accounts from Canada's Military History*. Toronto: Thomas Allen Publishers, 2004.

Gwyn, Sandra. *The Private Capital: Ambition and Love in the Age of Macdonald and Laurier*. Toronto: McClelland and Stewart Limited, 1984.

----------. *Tapestry of War: A Private View of Canadians in the Great War*. Toronto: HarperCollins, 1992.

Miller, Carman. *Painting the Map Red: Canada and the South African War, 1899-1902*. Montreal & Kingston: McGill-Queen's University Press, 1993. Canadian War Museum Historical Publication 28.

----------. "The Unhappy Warriors: Conflict and Nationality among the Canadian Troops during the South African War." *Journal of Imperial and Commonwealth History* 23, 1 (1995), 77-104.

Morton, Desmond. *A Military History of Canada*. 4th ed. Toronto: McClelland & Stewart Incorporated, 1999.

Steele, Samuel B. *Forty Years in Canada*. Toronto: McClelland, Goodchild & Stewart, 1914.

Glossary

CDA	Canadian Defence Academy
CFLI	Canadian Forces Leadership Institute
CLIP	Canadian Letters and Images Project
CMR	Canadian Mounted Rifles
CO	Commanding Officer
DCB	Dictionary of Canadian Biography
DSO	Distinguished Service Order
GGFG	Governor General's Foot Guards
LAC	Library and Archives Canada
LdSH	Lord Strathcona's Horse
MG	Manuscript Group
MP	Member of Parliament
NCO	Non-Commissioned Officer
NWMP	North-West Mounted Police
PPCLI	Princess Patricia's Canadian Light Infantry
RCRI	Royal Canadian Regiment of Infantry
RG	Record Group
SALH	South African Light Horse
SH	Strathcona's Horse
UTP	University of Toronto Press
VC	Victoria Cross
WO	War Office

Index

3rd (Special Service) Battalion, Royal Canadian Regiment of Infantry 15
6th Canadian Mounted Rifles 69, 72, **93** *notes*, 100
7th Brigade 6

"A Private in the Rear Ranks" (pseudonym) 17
Adamson, Agar Stewart Allan Masterson iii, v, 2-5, 7, **9** *notes*, 11-19, 22-37, 39-55, 57-62, 64, 65, 67-72, 76, **77-98** *notes*, 99-101
Adamson, James 12
Adamson, Mary Julia 12
Adamson, William Agar 12, **78** *notes*
Afghanistan 2
Amersfoort 55

Badfontein Valley 59
Belgium 6, 74
Bertram, Sergeant Instructor 33
Boers 37-42, 44-50, 52, 58, 59, 70, 73, **92** *notes*
Borden, Dr. Frederick William 20, 22, **78** *notes*, **81** *notes*, **82** *notes*, **96** *notes*
Bowers, George 52, 63, **87** *notes*, **91** *notes*, **94** *notes*
British Army 77
British Columbia 19, 21
Buller, General Sir Redvers 32
Byng, Colonel 68
Byng, Sir Julian 11, **96** *notes*

Calgary 21, **81** *notes*, 111
Cambridge 62
Canada iii-v, 1, 3, 5, **8** *notes*, **9** *notes*, 12, 22, 24, 29, 30, 32, 34, 37, 47, 52, 53, 64, 65, 67, 68, 71, 73, 75, **76** *notes*, **78-80** *notes*, **84** *notes*, **89** *notes*, **91** *notes*, **93-95** *notes*, 99, 100, **101** *biblio.*, 103
Canadian Corps 6, **7** *notes*, **8** *notes*, 96

Canadian Forces Leadership Institute vi, 1, 103, 111
Canadian High Commissioner in London 12
Canadian Military Gazette 17
Canadian militia 13, 14, 26, 68, 70, 73, **84** *notes*
Canadian Pacific Railway 24
Cape Town 28, 30, 64, 99
Carey, Lance-Corporal 36
Carolina 57
Cawthra, John 15, **79** *notes*
Cawthra, Ann Mabel 14, 22, **79** *notes*
Charleston 35, 50
Cleary, General 65
Corpus Christi 13
Crocodile Valley 58, **92** *notes*

Department of Militia and Defence **80** *notes*, **81** *notes*, **97** *notes*, **101** *biblio*.
Derbishire, Stewart 13
Devonshire Regiment 51
Distinguished Service Order 6, **8** *notes*, 73, 103
Durban 32, 52, 70, 100
dysentery 63

East London 32
Emerlo 57
England 3, 11, 13, 24-27, 64, **77** *notes*, **94** *notes*
enteric fever 63, **94** *notes*

First World War 6, **7** *notes*, **9** *notes*, 73-75, **76** *notes*, **86** *notes*, **90** *notes*, **96** *notes*, **98** *notes*
France 6, **7** *notes*, 64, 74

General Officer Commanding the Canadian Militia 13
Geological Survey 65
Germans 73
Glencoe 22

Gordon, Major W.D. 70
Government House 18, 66
Governor General 13, 14, 66, 79
Governor General's Foot Guards 13, 78, 103
Great Britain 63

Halifax 15-18, 23, 26, 30, 33, 64, 68, 70, **79** *notes*, **80** *notes*, **82-84** *notes*, 94 *notes*, 97 *notes*
Harrods 65
Hodgins, Lieutenant-Colonel W.E. 68
Howell, Thomas Easton 44-46, 57, 60, **83** *notes*, **86-88** *notes*, **90-93** *notes*
Hutton, Major-General E.T.H. 13, 14, 65, **78** *notes*, **82** *notes*
Hutton, Mrs. 65, **78** *notes*

In Harm's Way 1, **8** notes
Iraq 2
Irving, Lieutenant-Colonel J.D. 70

Jarvis, Lieutenant-Colonel A.L. 68, **97** *notes*

Keegan, Sir John 2, **8** *notes*

Lady Dudly 65
Lansdowne Park 23, 24, **83** *notes*
Leinster Regiment 15
Liverpool 27, 29
London **8** *notes*, **9** *notes*, 12, 23, 27, 29, 32, 64-66, **94** *notes*
Lord Ava 14, **79** *notes*
Lord Dufferin 14, **79** *notes*
Lord Dundonald 65, **91** *notes*
Lord Minto 13, 22, **78** *notes*, **83** *notes*
Lord Strathcona 12, 19, 25, 27, 28, 47, 52, 61, 65, 76, **78** *notes*, **88** *notes*, **89** *notes*, **95** *notes*, 99, 100, 103

Macdonald, Sir John A. 13
Macmillan, Frank 46
McArthur, Alex 41, 42, 44, 47, **89** *notes*
McGill University **8** *notes*, 46
McGillivray, Private 58, 60
Machadodorp 57, **92** *notes*, **93** *notes*
Maitland Camp 28, 32, 48, 54
Manitoba 19, **84** *notes*
Mason 57
Mexico 15
Miller, Andrew 46, **79** *notes*, **81** *notes*, **88** *notes*, **89** *notes*, **91** *notes*, **92** *notes*
Minister of Militia and Defence 20, 67, **78** *notes*
Montreal **8** *notes*, 24, **84** *notes*, **101** *biblio.*

Natal 32, **86** *notes*, **92** *notes*
Natal Field Force 32, **86** *notes*, **92** *notes*
Newmarket stakes 13, 27
Niagara 14
North-West Mounted Police 20, 103
North-West Rebellion (1885) 67
North-West Territories 19
Nova Scotia 15, **80** *notes*

Ottawa 13, 16, 19-21, 23-26, 30, 33, 37, 42, 65, **81** *notes*, **83** *notes*, 99, **101** *biblio.*

Paarde Kop 54, **91** *notes*
Paardeberg 66, **86** *notes*, 100
Port Elizabeth 32, 33
Port Hope 13
Powell, Chief 23
Princess Patricia's Canadian Light Infantry 6, **9** *notes*, 11, 100, 103
Provost-Marshal 52

Quebec 66
Queen Victoria 20

Reserve of Officers 71
Revelstoke 21, 81 notea
Richardson, Sergeant A.H.L. 5, 41, 42, 44, 47, 48, 67, 73, **89** *notes*
Royal Albert Docks 26

Senate of Canada 12
Ships 28
    Assaye 27, 28 **93** *notes*
    Idaho 32, 33
    Minnehaha 65
    Oratava 64
    Vancouver 24, 27
    Winifredian 70
Smith, Donald (See Lord Strathcona) 12, **78** *notes*
South Africa iii, 2, **8** *notes*, 19, 20, 27, 35, 37, 48, 49, 59, 63, 66, 71-73, 75, 76, **82** *notes*, **84** *notes*, **86** *notes*, **89** *notes*, **91** *notes*, **96** *notes*, 99
South African Light Horse 36, 46, 103
South African War iii, v, 3, 5, 6, **8** *notes*, 12, 72-73, **79** *notes*, **80** *notes*, **87** *notes*, **89** *notes*, **91** *notes*, **93** *notes*, **101** *biblio*, **102** *biblio*.
Sparkes, George 42, **84** *notes*, **89** *notes*
Speaker of the Senate 65
St. George's Church 15
St. Vincent 27, 29
Standerton 36-38, 41, 43, 46, 47
Steele, Lieutenant-Colonel Sam 20, 52-55, 61-63, 65, 68, 69, 76, **88** *notes*, **89** *notes*, **91-95** *notes*, **97** *notes*, **98** *notes*, 99, 100
Stewart, David Morrison 26, 28
Strathcona's Horse 3, 12, 18, 19, 24, 46, 56, 58, 61, 66, 68, 72, **78** *notes*, **80** *notes*, **83** *notes*, **86-91** *notes*, 99, 100, 103
Strickland, Inspector 20, 21, 24, **81** notes

Toller, Lieutenant-Colonel F.   68
Toronto   8 *notes*, 9 *notes*, 15, 86 *notes*, 99, 101 *biblio.*, 102 *biblio.*, 103
Trinity College   13
Trocadero   65

War Office   20, 78 notes, 81 notes, 103
Watervaal   52
Wellington Barracks   15, 80 *notes*
Western Front   11, 12
Winnipeg   9 *notes*, 21, 81 *notes*
Wolve Spruit   iii, 5, 37, 45, 47, 50, 51, 55, 88 *notes*

Vancouver   21, 81 *notes*
Victoria Cross   5, 37, 47, 73, 88 *notes*, 89 *notes*
Vidal, Lieutenant-Colonel   16
Vimy   11

Author's Biography

Craig Leslie Mantle, a doctoral candidate at the University of Calgary, graduated from Queen's University in 2002 with his Master of Arts degree in Canadian military history. From that time forward, he has been employed as a research officer by the Canadian Forces Leadership Institute in Kingston, Ontario. He is the editor of two books that explore both the theoretical underpinnings and historical aspects of disobedience in the Canadian military, and the co-editor of two books that examine the relationship between Aboriginal peoples and the military.